THE MIDDLE EAST IN TURMOIL

THE SANCTIONS SQUEEZE ON IRAN AND SYRIA

THE MIDDLE EAST IN TURMOIL

Additional books in this series can be found on Nova's website under the Series tab.

Additional E-books in this series can be found on Nova's website under the E-books tab.

GLOBAL POLITICAL STUDIES

Additional books in this series can be found on Nova's website under the Series tab.

Additional E-books in this series can be found on Nova's website under the E-books tab.

THE MIDDLE EAST IN TURMOIL

THE SANCTIONS SQUEEZE ON IRAN AND SYRIA

MITCH H. ROCHA
AND
RICKY L. PUCKETT
EDITORS

Nova Science Publishers, Inc.
New York

Library of Congress Cataloging-in-Publication Data

ISBN 978-1-62081-015-6

Published by Nova Science Publishers, Inc. † New York

CONTENTS

PREFACE

This book examines the broad international support for imposing progressively strict economic sanctions on Iran to try to compel it to verifiably confine its nuclear program to purely peaceful times. Additionally, this book analyzes the current unrest in Syria and the U.S. response to the Syrian government's crackdown against demonstrators, providing background information on U.S. sanctions against the Asad regime and its supporters.

Chapter 1- There is broad international support for imposing progressively strict economic sanctions on Iran to try to compel it to verifiably confine its nuclear program to purely peaceful uses.

Many U.S. and international officials appear to agree that the sanctions have not, to date, hurt Iran's economy to the point at which the Iranian leadership feels pressured to accommodate core Western goals on Iran's nuclear program.

As of September 2011, Iran's leaders have stated interest in new proposals that could form the basis of revived nuclear talks, although prospects for new talks have been set back by diplomatic rifts between Iran and several European countries in November 2011.

Whether or not core goals have yet been accomplished, the United States and its allies appear to agree that sanctions might yet succeed and that pressure should be added to further weaken Iran's energy sector and isolate Iran from the international financial system. The energy sector provides nearly 70% of government revenues.

Iran's large trading community needs financing to buy goods from the West and sell them inside Iran. There have been a stream of announcements by major international firms since early 2010 that they are exiting or declining to undertake further work in the Iranian market, particularly the energy sector, taking with them often irreplaceable expertise. Partly as a result, Iran's oil production has remained relatively steady at about 4.1 million barrels per day, defying Iranian efforts to increase production.

Chapter 2- This report analyzes the unrest in Syria and the U.S. response to the Syrian government's crackdown against demonstrators. It also provides background information on U.S. sanctions against the Asad regime and its supporters.

A variety of U.S. legislative provisions and executive directives prohibit direct foreign assistance funding to Syria and restrict bilateral trade relations, largely because of the U.S. State Department's designation of Syria as a sponsor of international terrorism. On December 12, 2003, President George W. Bush signed the Syria Accountability Act, P.L. 108-175, which imposed additional economic sanctions against Syria. Syrian individuals and government officials are subject to targeted financial sanctions pursuant to executive orders relating to terrorism, proliferation, and regional security. Successive administrations have designated several Syrian entities as weapons proliferators and sanctioned several Russian companies for alleged weapons of mass destruction or advanced weapons sales to Syria.

The following legislation introduced in the 112th Congress addresses the current situation in Syria.

H.R. 2106, The Syria Freedom Support Act. Sanctions the development of petroleum resources of Syria, the production of refined petroleum products in Syria, and the exportation of refined petroleum products to Syria.

H.Res. 296 (S.Res. 180 in the Senate). Expresses support for peaceful demonstrations and universal freedoms in Syria and condemns the human rights violations by the Assad Regime.

H.R. 2105, The Iran, North Korea, and Syria Nonproliferation Reform and Modernization Act of 2011. States that it shall be U.S. policy to fully implement and enforce sanctions against Iran, North Korea, and Syria for their proliferation activities and policies.

S. 1048, The Iran, North Korea, and Syria Sanctions Consolidation Act of 2011. Amends the Iran, North Korea, and Syria Nonproliferation Act to include in the scope of such act a person that (1) acquired materials mined or extracted within North Korea's territory or control; or (2) provided shipping services for the transportation of goods to or from Iran, North Korea, or Syria relating to such countries' weapons of mass destruction programs, support for acts of international terrorism, or human rights abuses. Excludes from such provisions shipping services for emergency or humanitarian purposes.

S. 1472, The Syria Sanctions Act of 2011. Denies companies that conduct business in Syria's energy sector (investment, oil purchases, and sale of gasoline) access to U.S. financial institutions and requires federal contractors to certify that they are not engaged in sanctionable activity.

In: The Sanctions Squeeze on Iran and Syria ISBN: 978-1- 62081-015-6
Editors: M. H. Rocha and R. L. Puckett

Chapter 1

IRAN SANCTIONS*

Kenneth Katzman

SUMMARY

There is broad international support for imposing progressively strict economic sanctions on Iran to try to compel it to verifiably confine its nuclear program to purely peaceful uses.

Many U.S. and international officials appear to agree that the sanctions have not, to date, hurt Iran's economy to the point at which the Iranian leadership feels pressured to accommodate core Western goals on Iran's nuclear program.

As of September 2011, Iran's leaders have stated interest in new proposals that could form the basis of revived nuclear talks, although prospects for new talks have been set back by diplomatic rifts between Iran and several European countries in November 2011.

Whether or not core goals have yet been accomplished, the United States and its allies appear to agree that sanctions might yet succeed and that pressure should be added to further weaken Iran's energy sector and isolate Iran from the international financial system. The energy sector provides nearly 70% of government revenues.

Iran's large trading community needs financing to buy goods from the West and sell them inside Iran. There have been a stream of announcements by major international firms since early 2010 that they

* This is an edited, reformatted and augmented version of a Congressional Research Service publication, CRS Report for Congress RS20871, from www.crs.gov, prepared for Members and Committees of Congress, dated December 2, 2011.

are exiting or declining to undertake further work in the Iranian market, particularly the energy sector, taking with them often irreplaceable expertise. Partly as a result, Iran's oil production has remained relatively steady at about 4.1 million barrels per day, defying Iranian efforts to increase production.

Iran has small amounts of natural gas exports; it had none at all before Iran opened its fields to foreign investment in 1996.

Several countries, particularly India, have delayed billions of dollars in oil payments for Iran because payments mechanisms have been disrupted by sanctions.

However, Iran's overall ability to limit the effects of sanctions has been aided by relatively high oil prices in 2011.

What has generated U.S. optimism about the eventual success of sanctions has been the broadening of international support for and compliance with them.

Using the authorities of U.N. Security Council Resolution 1929, adopted June 9, 2010, measures adopted since mid-2010 by the United Nations Security Council, the European Union, and several other countries target the key energy and financial sectors of Iran.

These measures complement the numerous U.S. laws and regulations that have long sought to try to pressure Iran, particularly the Iran Sanctions Act (ISA)—a 1996 U.S. law that mandates U.S. penalties against foreign companies that invest in Iran's energy sector.

The application of that law was broadened by the Comprehensive Iran Sanctions, Accountability, and Divestment Act of 2010 (CISADA, P.L. 111-195) as well as by Executive Order 13590 issued November 21, 2011.

The issuing of that Order was accompanied by a Treasury Department warning, under Section 311 of the USA Patriot Act, that conducting transactions with the Iranian financial system constitutes a risk of facilitating Iranian proliferation and terrorism financing activity.

The prospects for additional international sanctions have been heightened in late 2011 by U.S. revelations in October 2011 of a purported Iranian plot to assassinate the Saudi Ambassador to the United States, an International Atomic Energy Agency (IAEA) report on Iran's possible efforts to design a nuclear explosive device, and diplomatic and financial rifts with Britain, which caused the storming of the British Embassy in Tehran on November 30, 2011.

In the 112th Congress, legislation, such as S. 1048 and H.R. 1905, would enhance both the economic sanctions and human rights-related provisions of CISADA and other laws. An amendment to a Senate FY2012 defense authorization bill would sanction foreign banks that do business with Iran's Central Bank. Some countries and experts also seek a broad or partial embargo on Iran's sale of oil, to reinforce the sanctions effects discussed above.

Overview

The Obama administration's policy approach toward Iran has contrasted with the Bush administration's by attempting to couple the imposition of sanctions to U.S. negotiations with Iran on the nuclear issue. However, with negotiations yielding no firm Iranian agreement to compromise, since early 2010 the administration and Congress have focused on achieving adoption of and implementing additional U.S., U.N., and allied country sanctions whose cumulative effect could compel Iran to accept a nuclear bargain.

U.N. and worldwide bilateral sanctions on Iran (the latest of which are imposed by Resolution 1929, adopted June 9, 2010) are a relatively recent (post-2006) development. U.S. sanctions, on the other hand, have been a major feature of U.S. Iran policy since Iran's 1979 Islamic revolution. Many of the U.S. sanctions overlap each other as well as the U.N. sanctions now in place, and national measures undertaken by European and some Asian countries. Some U.S. sanctions, particularly the 1996 Iran Sanctions Act (ISA), caused differences of opinion between the United States and its European allies because it mandates U.S. imposition of sanctions on foreign firms. Successive administrations have sought to ensure that U.S. sanctions do not hamper cooperation with key international partners whose support is needed to isolate Iran.

Sanctions Targeting Foreign Participation in Iran's Energy Sector: The Iran Sanctions Act (ISA), CISADA, and a November 2011 Executive Order

The Iran Sanctions Act (ISA) is one of many U.S. sanctions in place against Iran. It has attracted substantial attention because it is an "extra-territorial sanction"—it authorizes U.S. penalties against foreign firms, many of which are incorporated in countries that are U.S. allies. When it was first enacted in 1996, Congress and the Clinton administration saw ISA as a potential mechanism to compel U.S. allies to join the United States in enacting trade sanctions against Iran. American firms are separately restricted from trading with or investing in Iran under separate U.S. executive orders, as discussed below. Its application has been further expanded by CISADA (P.L. 111-195) as well as by Executive Order 13590, issued November 21, 2011.

Originally called the Iran and Libya Sanctions Act (ILSA), ISA was enacted to try to deny Iran the resources to further its nuclear program and to support terrorist organizations such as Hizbollah, Hamas, and Palestine Islamic Jihad. Iran's petroleum sector generates about 20% of Iran's GDP (which is about $870 billion), 80% of its exports, and 70% of its government revenue. Iran's oil sector is as old as the petroleum industry itself (early 20th century), and Iran's onshore oil fields and oil industry infrastructure are far past peak production and in need of substantial investment. Its large natural gas resources (940 trillion cubic feet, exceeded only by Russia) were virtually undeveloped when ISA was first enacted. Iran has 136.3 billion barrels of proven oil reserves, the third-largest after Saudi Arabia and Canada.

Legislative History and Provisions

The opportunity for the United States to try to harm Iran's energy sector came in November 1995, when Iran opened the sector to foreign investment. To accommodate its insistence on retaining control of its national resources, Iran used a "buy-back" investment program in which foreign firms gradually recoup their investments as oil and gas is discovered and then produced. With input from the administration, on September 8, 1995, Senator Alfonse D'Amato introduced the "Iran Foreign Oil Sanctions Act" to sanction foreign firms' exports to Iran of energy technology. A revised version instead sanctioning *investment* in Iran's energy sector passed the Senate on December 18, 1995 (voice vote). On December 20, 1995, the Senate passed a version applying the provisions to Libya, which was refusing to yield for trial the two intelligence agents suspected in the December 21, 1988, bombing of Pan Am 103. The House passed H.R. 3107, on June 19, 1996 (415-0), and then concurred on a Senate version adopted on July 16, 1996 (unanimous consent). The Iran and Libya Sanctions Act was signed on August 5, 1996 (P.L. 104-172).

Key "Triggers"

ISA consists of a number of "triggers" - transactions with Iran that would be considered violations of ISA and could cause a firm or entity to be sanctioned under ISA's provisions. When triggered, ISA provides a number of different sanctions that the president could impose that would harm a foreign firm's business opportunities in the United States. ISA does not, and probably could not practically, compel any foreign government to act against one of its firms.

Original Triggers

ISA primarily targets foreign firms, because American firms are already prohibited from investing in Iran under the 1995 trade and investment ban discussed below. The original version of ISA requires the president to sanction companies (entities, persons) that make an "investment"[1] of more than $20 million[2] in one year in Iran's energy sector.[3] The definition of "investment" in ISA (Section 14 (9)) includes not only equity and royalty arrangements (including additions to existing investment, as added by P.L. 107-24) but any contract that includes "responsibility for the development of petroleum resources" of Iran.

CISADA did not alter this trigger but it did amend the definition of investment to include pipelines to or through Iran and contracts to lead the construction, upgrading, or expansions of energy projects. CISADA also eliminated the wording in the original version of ISA thatspecifically exempts from sanctions sales of energy-related equipment to Iran. However, to be sanctionable, such sales would need to be structured as investments or ongoing profit-earning ventures rather than simple sales transactions.

The Iran Freedom Support Act (P.L. 109-293) amended ISA to add a trigger: that sanctions should be imposed on entities that sell to Iran weapons of mass destruction (WMD) technology or "destabilizing numbers and types" of advanced conventional weapons.

CISADA: Amended ISA by Adding a Trigger—Sales to Iran of Gasoline and Related Equipment and Services

ISA, as initially constituted, did not address Iran's gasoline dependency because sales to Iran of gasoline were not sanctionable under ISA. Nor did the original version sanction the selling to Iran of equipment with which it can build or expand its refineries using its own construction capabilities.[4] Nor did ISA clearly apply to Iranian investments in oil refineries in several other countries, such as Iranian investment to help build five oil refineries in Asia (China, Indonesia, Malaysia, and Singapore) and in Syria, reported in June 2007, would have constituted "investment" under ISA.

Many in Congress argued that ISA should be applied to gasoline sales to Iran because Iran is dependent on gasoline imports to meet about 40% of its gasoline needs and there were a limited group of major gasoline suppliers to Iran. Others, however, believed the Iranian government would have numerous ways to circumvent its effects, including rationing, reducing gasoline subsidies in an effort to reduce gasoline consumption; or offering premium prices to obscure gasoline suppliers. The effect on Iran's supplies are discussed later in this report.

Main CISADA Provision on Gasoline. CISADA's main provision was to amend ISA by making sanctionable:

- Sales to Iran of over $1 million worth (or $5 million in a one year period) of gasoline and related aviation and other fuels. (Fuel oil, a petroleum by-product which is reportedly being sold to Iran by exporters in the Kurdish region of Iraq, is not included in the definition of refined petroleum.)
- Sales to Iran of equipment or services which would help Iran make or import gasoline. Such sales would include equipment and services that Iran can use to construct or maintain its oil refineries.

In terms of legislative history, the ideas that became the core of CISADA were introduced as legislation in the 110th and 111th Congresses. In the 110th Congress, H.R. 2880 would have made sales to Iran of refined petroleum resources a violation of ISA.

In the 111th Congress, a House bill (Iran Refined Petroleum Sanctions Act) containing the provisions above sanctioning gasoline related sales to Iran, H.R. 2194, was passed by the House on December 15, 2009, by a vote of 412-12, with four others voting "present" and six others not voting. A bill in the Senate, the "Dodd-Shelby Comprehensive Iran Sanctions, Accountability, and Divestment Act," (S. 2799), was reported to the full Senate by the Senate Banking Committee on November 19, 2009, and passed the Senate, by voice vote, on January 28, 2010. It was adopted by the Senate under unanimous consent as a substitute amendment to H.R. 2194 on March 11, 2010, setting up conference action on the two versions of H.R. 2194. The Senate bill added to the House bill provisions affecting U.S.-Iran trade and other issues. As shown in *Table 2,* the final version contained many of the extensive provisions of the Senate version, and some of the efforts to compel sanctions represented in the House version. The president signed the final version on July 1, 2010 (P.L. 111-195).

Earlier in the 111th Congress, a few initiatives to sanction sales of gasoline to Iran were adopted prior to CSIDA. Using U.S. funds to fill the Strategic Petroleum Reserve with products from firms that sell over $1 million worth of gasoline to Iran is prevented by the FY2010 Energy and Water Appropriation

(H.R. 3183, P.L. 111-85, signed October 28, 2009). A provision of the FY2010 consolidated appropriation (P.L. 111-117) would deny Ex-Im Bank credits to any firm that sells gasoline to Iran, provides equipment to Iran that it can use to expand its oil refinery capabilities, or performs gasoline production projects in Iran.

These initiatives did deter some gasoline sales to Iran, including a decision in December 2008 by Reliance Industries Ltd. of India to at least temporarily cease new sales of refined gasoline to Iran (December 31, 2008). That decision came after several Members of Congress urged the Ex-Im Bank of the United States to suspend assistance to Reliance, on the grounds that it was assisting Iran's economy with the gas sales. The Ex-Im Bank, in August 2008, had extended a total of $900 million in financing guarantees to Reliance to help it expand.

Additional Triggers Added by Executive Order 13590 of November 21, 2011: Application of ISA to Sales of Energy Sector (Including Petrochemical) Equipment and Services

In the wake of a November 8, 2011, IAEA report indicating Iran might have worked on nuclear explosive technology, the administration issued an Executive Order, under the International Emergency Economic Powers Act (IEEPA), expanding the authorities of the Iran Sanctions Act to direct the Secretary of State to impose at least one (1) of the available ISA sanctions on foreign firms that:

- Provide to Iran $1 million or more (or $5 million in a one year period) worth of goods or services that Iran could use to maintain or enhance its oil and gas sector. This would appear to make sanctionable the activity of global oil services firms in Iran, or the provision to Iran of gear typically used in the oil industry such as drills, pumps, vacuums, oil rigs, and the like.
- Provide to Iran $250,000 (or $1 million in a one year period) worth of goods or services that Iran could use to maintain or expand its production of petrochemical products.
- Because these provisions were issued by Executive Order, the other legislative provisions of ISA, such as the time frame to begin and complete investigations of suspected violations, do not necessarily apply.

Mandate and Time Frame to Investigate Violations

In the original version of ISA, there was no firm requirement, and no time limit, for the administration to investigate potential violations and determine that a firm has violated ISA's provisions. Some might argue that the CISADA amendments still do not set a binding determination deadline, although the parameters are narrowed significantly.

In restricting the administration's ability to choose not to act on information about potential violations, CISADA, Section 102(g)(5), makes mandatory that the administration begin an investigation of potential ISA violations when there is "credible information" about a potential violation. The same section of CISADA makes mandatory the 180-day time limit for a determination of violation (with the exception that the mandatory investigations and time limit go into effect one year after enactment (as of July 1, 2011), with respect to gasoline related sales to Iran). Under Section 102(h)(5), the mandate to investigate gasoline related sales can be delayed an additional 180 days if an administration report, submitted to Congress by June 1, 2011, asserts that its policies have produced a significant result in sales of gasoline to Iran. No such report was submitted. However, there is still lack of precision and potential differences of opinion over what constitutes "credible information" that an investment or sanctionable sale has been undertaken.

Earlier, P.L. 109-293, the "Iran Freedom Support Act" (signed September 30, 2006) amended ISA by calling for, *but not requiring*, a 180-day time limit for a violation determination (there is no time limit in the original law).[5] Early versions of legislation (H.R. 282, S. 333) that ultimately became the Iran Freedom Support Act (P.L. 109-293) contained ISA amendment proposals that were viewed by the Bush administration as too inflexible and restrictive, and potentially harmful to U.S. relations with its allies. These provisions included setting a mandatory 90-day time limit for the administration to determine whether an investment is a violation; cutting U.S. foreign assistance to countries whose companies violate ISA; and applying the U.S.-Iran trade ban to foreign subsidiaries of U.S. firms.

Available Sanctions under ISA

Once a firm is determined to be a violator, the original version of ISA required the imposition of *two* of a menu of six sanctions on that firm. CISADA added three new possible sanctions and requires the imposition of at least *three out of the nine* against violators. Executive Order 13590, discussed above, provides for exactly the same penalties as those in ISA. The nine available sanctions against the sanctioned entity that the Secretary of State or of Treasury can select from (Section 6) include:

1) denial of Export-Import Bank loans, credits, or credit guarantees for U.S. exports to the sanctioned entity;
2) denial of licenses for the U.S. export of military or militarily useful technology to the entity;
3) denial of U.S. bank loans exceeding $10 million in one year to the entity;
4) if the entity is a financial institution, a prohibition on its service as a primary dealer in U.S. government bonds; and/or a prohibition on its serving as a repository for U.S. government funds (each counts as one sanction);
5) prohibition on U.S. government procurement from the entity;
6) prohibitions in transactions in foreign exchange by the entity;
7) prohibition on any credit or payments between the entity and any U.S. financial institution;
8) prohibition of the sanctioned entity from acquiring, holding, using, or trading any U.S.-based property which the sanctioned entity has a (financial) interest in; and
9) restriction on imports from the sanctioned entity, in accordance with the International Emergency Economic Powers Act (IEEPA, 50 USC. 1701).

New Mandatory ISA Sanction Imposed by CISADA: Prohibition on Contracts with the U.S. Government

CISADA (Section 102(b)) added a provision to further incent foreign companies to comply with ISA. It requires companies, as a condition of obtaining a U.S. government contract, to certify to the relevant U.S. government agency, that the firm—*and any companies it owns or controls*—are not violating ISA, as amended. A contract may be terminated—and further penalties imposed—if it is determined that the company's certification of compliance was false. CISADA requires a revision of the Federal Acquisition Regulation (within 90 days of CISADA enactment on July 1, 2010) to reflect this requirement.

This requirement has been imposed in regulations, as per an interim rule issued on September 29, 2010. H.R. 6296, introduced September 29, 2010, in the 111th Congress, would have authorized state and local governments to ban such contracts.

This sanction is not specified as available to apply to any firm sanctioned under Executive Order 13590.

Waivers, Exemptions, and Termination Authority

The president has had the authority under ISA to waive sanctions if he certifies that doing so is *important* to the U.S. national interest (Section 9(c)). CISADA (Section 102(c)), changed the 9(c) ISA waiver standard to "*necessary*" to the national interest. Under the original version of ISA, there was also waiver authority (Section 4(c)) if the parent country of the violating firm joined a sanctions regime against Iran, but this waiver provision was changed by the Iran Freedom Support Act (P.L. 109-293) to allow for a waiver determination based on U.S. vital national security interests. The Section 4(c) waiver was altered by CISADA to provide for a six month (extendable) waiver if doing so is vital to the national interest and if the parent country of the violating entity is "closely cooperating" with U.S. efforts against Iran's WMD and advanced conventional weapons program. The criteria of "closely cooperating" are defined in the conference report, with primary focus on implementing all U.N. sanctions against Iran. However, it is not clear why an administration would use a Section 4 waiver rather than a Section 9 waiver, although it could be argued that using a Section 4 waiver would support U.S. diplomacy with the parent country of the offending entity.

ISA (Section5(f)) also contains several exceptions such that the president is not required to impose sanctions that prevent procurement of defense articles and services under existingcontracts, in cases where a firm is the sole source supplier of a particular defense article or service. The president also is not required to prevent procurement or importation of essential spare parts or component parts.

In the 110th Congress, several bills not adopted contained provisions that would have further amended ISA; H.R. 1400, which passed the House on September 25, 2007 (397-16), would have removed the administration's ability to waive ISA sanctions under Section 9(c), national interest grounds, although without imposing a time limit for a sanctions determination.

"Special Rule" Exempting Firms That End Their Business with Iran

CISADA (Section 102(g)(5) amended ISA to provide a means—a so-called "special rule"—for firms to avoid any possibility of U.S. sanctions by pledging to verifiably end their business with Iran and to forgo any sanctionable business with Iran in the future. Under the special rule, the administration is not required to make a determination of sanctionability against a firm that makes such pledges. The special rule has been invoked on several occasions as discussed below.

Termination Requirements and Sunset Provisions

In its entirety, ISA application to Iran would terminate if Iran is determined by the administration to have ceased its efforts to acquire WMD; is removed from the U.S. list of state sponsors of terrorism; *and* no longer "poses a significant threat" to U.S. national security and U.S. allies.[6] The amendments to ISA made by P.L. 111-195 would terminate if the first two criteria are met.

Even without such determinations, ISA was to sunset on August 5, 2001, in a climate of lessening tensions with Iran (and Libya). During 1999 and 2000, the Clinton administration had eased the trade ban on Iran somewhat to try to engage the relatively moderate Iranian President Mohammad Khatemi. However, some maintained that Iran would view its expiration as a concession, and renewal legislation was enacted (P.L. 107-24, August 3, 2001). This law required an administration report on ISA's effectiveness within 24 to 30 months of enactment; that report was submitted to Congress in January 2004 and did not recommend that ISA be repealed. ISA was scheduled to sunset on December 31, 2011 (as provided by P.L. 109-293). The sunset is now December 31, 2016, as provided for in CISADA.

Interpretations and Implementation

The Obama administration has, as of 2010, stepped up U.S. efforts to use ISA authorities to discourage investment in Iran and to impose sanctions on companies that insist on continuing their business with Iran. This is a contrast from the first 10-15 years after ISA's passage, in which successive administrations hesitated to confront partner countries over its implementation.

Traditionally reticent to impose economic sanctions, the European Union opposed ISA, when it was first enacted, as an extraterritorial application of U.S. law. It threatened to file a formal complaint before the World Trade Organization (WTO). In April 1997, the United States and the EU agreed to avoid a trade confrontation over ISA and a separate Cuba sanctions law (P.L. 104- 114).

The agreement involved the promise by the EU not to file any complaint with the WTO over this issue, in exchange for the eventual May 18, 1998, announcement by the Clinton administration to waive ISA sanctions ("national interest"—Section 9c—waiver) on the first project determined to be in violation. That project was a $2 billion[7] contract, signed in September 1997, for Total SA of France and its partners, Gazprom of Russia and Petronas of Malaysia, to develop phases 2 and 3 of the 25+ phase South Pars gas field. The EU, for its part, pledged to increase cooperation with the United States on nonproliferation and counterterrorism. Then-Secretary of State Albright, in the May 18, 1998, waiver announcement, indicated that similar future such projects by EU firms in Iran would not be sanctioned, provided overall EU cooperation against Iranian terrorism and proliferation continued.[8] (The EU sanctions against Iran, announced July 27, 2010, might render this understanding moot because the EU sanctions ban EU investment in and supplies of equipment and services to Iran's energy sector.) Despite investments made in Iran's energy sector, as shown in *Table 5*, the administration made no violations determinations from 1998 until September 2010.

ISA Sanctions Determinations: September 2010 to the Present[9]

Prior to the passage of CISADA, several Members of Congress questioned why no penalties had been imposed for violations of ISA. State Department reports to Congress on ISA, required every six months, have routinely stated that U.S. diplomats raise U.S. policy concerns about Iran with investing companies and their parent countries. However, these reports have not specifically stated which foreign companies, if any, were being investigated for ISA violations. No publication of such deals has been placed in the *Federal Register,* as required by Section 5e of ISA. In an effort to address the congressional criticism, Under Secretary of State for Political Affairs William Burns testified on July 9, 2008 (House Foreign Affairs Committee), that the Statoil project (listed in *Table 6*) was under review for ISA sanctions. Statoil is incorporated in Norway, which is not an EU member, and it would therefore not fall under the 1998 U.S.-EU agreement discussed above.

Possibly in response to the pending CISADA legislation, and to an October 2009 letter signed by 50 Members of Congress referencing *Table 5*, Assistant Secretary of State for Near Eastern Affairs Jeffrey Feltman testified before the House Foreign Affairs Committee on October 28, 2009, that the Obama administration would review investments in Iran for violations of ISA. Feltman testified that the preliminary review would be completed within 45 days (by December 11, 2009) to determine which projects, if any, require further investigation. He testified that some announced projects were for political purposes and did not result in actual investment.

On February 25, 2010, Secretary of State Clinton testified before the House Foreign Affairs Committee that the State Department's preliminary review was completed in early February and that some of the cases reviewed "deserve[] more consideration" and were undergoing additional scrutiny. The preliminary review, according to the testimony, was conducted, in part, throughState Department officials' contacts with their counterpart officials abroad and corporation officials. The additional investigations of problematic investments would involve the intelligence community, according to Secretary Clinton. State Department officials told CRS in November 2009 that they intended to complete the additional investigation and determine violations within 180 days of the completion of the preliminary review, or by early August 2010. (The 180-day time frame was, according to the Department officials, consistent with the Iran Freedom Support Act amendments to ISA discussed above, even though the 180-day time frame was not a mandatory deadline before CISADA was adopted.) On June 22, 2010, then Assistant Secretary of State William Burns testified before the Senate Foreign Relations Committee that there were "less than 10" cases of possible ISA violations.

September 30, 2010, Sanctions Determinations

Several determinations of sanctionability were made on September 30, 2010. That day, a Swiss-based Iranian-owned oil trading company—Naftiran Intertrade Company (NICO)—became the first firm to be sanctioned under ISA. The three penalties selected were: a ban on Ex-Im Bank credits; a denial of dual use export licensing to the firm; and a denial of bank loans exceeding $10 million. The mandatory ban on receiving U.S. government contracts applies as well.

That same day, following a months-long administration review discussed later, four major energy sector investing companies were deemed eligible to avoid sanctions, under the ISA "special rule," by pledging to end their business in Iran. They are

- Total of France,
- Statoil of Norway,
- ENI of Italy, and
- Royal Dutch Shell of Britain and the Netherlands.
- Inpex of Japan was exempted from sanctions under the special rule on November 17, 2010, according to a State Department announcement. The firm announced on October 15, 2010, that it is shedding its stake in the Azadegan development project shown in the table.

There remained some difference of opinion on the administration invocation of the special rule, as evident at a hearing of the House Foreign Affairs Committee on December 1, 2010. At the hearing, then Under Secretary Burns stated that companies exempted under the special rule had pledged to end their existing investments in Iran "in the very near future." Some Members of Congress questioned the imprecision of that time frame and others question the process for determining whether a firm is adhering to its pledge to pursue no future business in Iran's energy sector. The energy firms insisted they needed time to wind down their investments in Iran—under the buy-back program used for investments in Iran, the energy firms are paid back their investment over time, making it highly costly for them to suddenly end operations in Iran.

March 29, 2011, Sanctions Determination against Belarusneft

As shown in *Table 5,* several additional foreign investment agreements have been agreed with Iran not covered in the September 2010 determination. Some of these firms remained under administration scrutiny, and the administration stated that determinations will be made within 180 days (by April 1, 2011).

On March 29, 2011, with that deadline approaching, the StateDepartment announced that one additional firm would be sanctioned under ISA—Belarusneft, a subsidiary of the Belarus government owned Belneftekhim—for a $500 million contract with Naftiran (the company sanctioned in September 2010) to develop the Jofeir oil field discussed in *Table 5.* Other subsidiaries of Belneftekhim were sanctioned in 2007 under Executive Order 13405 related to U.S. policy on Belarus. The three ISA sanctions imposed on March 29, 2011, were denial of Exim Bank financing, denial of U.S. export licenses, and denial of U.S. loans above $10 million.

The administration announcement did not indicate that some of the other investments in *Table 5* or other investments, for which no ISA determinations have been made to date, are still under investigation. In public statements and letters to the administration, some Members of Congress have expressed concern that Chinese firms have not been sanctioned, indicating that the administration might be emphasizing some policy goals with respect to China at the expense of implementing sanctions against Iran.

May 24, 2011, Sanctions Imposed on Gasoline-Related Exportation to Iran

On May 24, 2011, the administration issued its first sanctions determinations under the CISADAamended "trigger" that requires sanctions against sales of gasoline and related equipment and services. The reasons for the sanctions, including size of gasoline shipments to Iran, as well as the ISA-related sanctions selected, can be found at http://www.state.gov /r/pa/prs/ ps/2011/05/ 164132.htm. The seven firms sanctioned were:

- Petrochemical Commercial Company International (PCCI) of Bailiwick of Jersey and Iran
- Royal Oyster Group (UAE)
- Tanker Pacific (Singapore)
- Allvale Maritime (subsidiary of Ofer Brothers Group, Israel)
- Societie Anonyme Monegasque Et Aerienne (SAMAMA, Monaco, subsidiary of Ofer Brothers)
- Speedy Ship (UAE/Iran)
- Associated Shipbroking (Monaco)
- Petroleos de Venezuela (PDVSA) of Venezuela

The determinations of sanctionability of Allvale and SAMAMA were issued on September 13, 2011, as a "clarification" of the May 24 determinations, which named Ofer Brothers Group (and not Allvale or SAMAMA) as sanctioned entities at that time. Ofer Brothers Group, the parent company in Israel, is not therefore under sanction Many of the firms sanctioned on May 24, 2011, including the two "clarified" as added on September 13, were subjected to the financial-related sanctions provided in ISA.

With respect to PDVSA, the administration made clear in its announcement that U.S.-based subsidiaries were not included in the determination and that U.S. purchases of Venezuelan oil would not be affected. The day prior to the May 2011 sanctions announcement, President Obama issued an executive order clarifying that it is the responsibility of the Treasury Department to implement those ISA sanctions that involve the financial sector, including bans on loans, credits, and foreign exchange for, or imports from the sanctioned entity, as well as blockage of property of the sanctioned entity (if these sanctions are selected by the Secretary of State, who makes the decision which penalties to impose on sanctioned entities).

Non-Application to Crude Oil or Natural Gas Purchases from Iran or to Official Credit Guarantee Agencies

Simple purchases of oil or natural gas from Iran are generally considered not to constitute violations of ISA, because ISA sanctions *investment* in Iran's energy sector and sales to Iran of gasoline or gasoline-related services or equipment. Some of the deals listed in the chart later in this report involve *combinations* of investment and purchase.

However, as discussed later, many experts are looking at trying to sanction such purchases of crude oil or natural gas as the optimal means of pressuring Iran's economy.

As noted above, ISA itself does not sanction sales to Iran of equipment that Iran could use to explore or extract its own oil or gas resources, *unless such sales are structured to provide ongoing profits or royalties (and therefore meet the definition of investments as provided in ISA*).[10]

For example, selling Iran an oil or gas drill rig or motors or other gear that Iran will use to drill for oil or gas would not appear to be sanctionable under ISA, unless the sale is structured to provide the seller ongoing profits or royalties. However, this exception was made moot by Executive Order 13590, issued November 21, 2011, which does provide for sanctions against sales of such equipment and services.

Official credit guarantee agencies are not considered sanctionable entities under ISA. In the 110th Congress, several bills—including S. 970, S. 3227, S. 3445, H.R. 957 (passed the House on July 31, 2007), and H.R. 7112 (which passed the House on September 26, 2008)—would have expanded the definition of sanctionable entities to official credit guarantee agencies, such as France's COFACE and Germany's Hermes, and to financial institutions and insurers generally. Some versions of CISADA would have made these entities sanctionable but these provisions were not included in the final law, probably out of concern for alienating U.S. allies in Europe.

Application to Energy Pipelines

As noted earlier, ISA's definition of sanctionable "investment," which specifies investment in Iran's petroleum resources, defined as petroleum and natural gas, has been interpreted by successive administrations to include construction of energy pipelines to or through Iran.

That interpretation was reinforced by amendments to ISA in CISADA, which specifically included in the definition of petroleum resources "products used to construct or maintain pipelines used to transport oil or liquefied natural gas."

The Clinton and Bush administrations used the threat of ISA sanctions to deter oil routes involving Iran and thereby successfully promoted an alternate route from Azerbaijan (Baku) to Turkey (Ceyhan). The route became operational in 2005.

Table 1. Major Energy Buyers From Iran (2010)
(amounts in millions of U.S. dollars; includes mineral fuels, crude oil, natural gas, distillates, and the like)

South Africa	22,855
China	13,044
Japan	11,030
India	9,394
Turkey	6,642
South Korea	6,447
Italy	5,763
Spain	4,348
Netherlands	2,608
Taiwan	2,162
Singapore	2,152
Greece	1,520
France	1,036
Germany	788
Sri Lanka	645
Austria	370
Indonesia	370
Malaysia	332
United Kingdom	226
Australia	138
Portugal	133
Thailand	129
Morocco	121
Czech Republic	89
Brazil	60

Source: World Trade Atlas, adapted by Susan Chesser, Knowledge Services Group, CRS.

Only a few significant pipelines involving Iran have been constructed in recent years—a line built in 1997 to carry natural gas from Iran to Turkey.

Each country constructed the pipeline on its side of their border. At the time the project was under construction, State Department testimony stated that Turkey would be importing gas originating in Turkmenistan, not Iran, under a swap arrangement. That was one reason given for why the State Department did not determine that the project was sanctionable under ISA. However, many believe the decision not to sanction the pipeline was because the line was viewed as crucial to Turkey, a key U.S. ally. That explanation was reinforced when direct Iranian gas exports to Turkey through the line began in 2001, and no determination of sanctionability has been made. In May 2009, Iran and Armenia inaugurated a natural gas pipeline between the two, built by Gazprom of Russia. No determination of sanctionability has been announced.

As shown in *Table 5*, in July 2007, a preliminary agreement was reached to build a second Iran-Turkey pipeline, through which Iranian gas would also flow to Europe. That agreement was not finalized during Iranian President Mahmoud Ahmadinejad's visit to Turkey in August 2008 because of Turkish commercial concerns, but the deal reportedly remains under discussion. On February 23, 2009, Iranian newspapers said Iran had formed a joint venture with a Turkish firm to export 35 billion cubic meters of gas per year to Europe; 50% of the venture would be owned by the National Iranian Gas Export Company (NIGEC).

Iran and Kuwait have held talks on the construction of a 350-mile pipeline that would bring Iranian gas to Kuwait. The two sides have apparently reached agreement on volumes (8.5 million cubic meters of gas would go to Kuwait each day) but not on price.[11] There are also discussions reported between Iran and Iraq on constructing pipelines to facilitate oil and gas swaps between the two, but no firm movement on these projects is evident.

Iran-Pakistan- India Pipeline (IPI)

Another pending pipeline project would carry Iranian gas, by pipeline, to Pakistan. India had been a part of the $7 billion project, which would take about three years to complete, but India it did not sign a memorandum between Iran and Pakistan finalizing the deal on June 12, 2010. India reportedly has been concerned about the security of the pipeline, the location at which the gas would be officially transferred to India, pricing of the gas, tariffs, and the source in Iran of the gas to be sold. Other steps taken by India since late 2010 to prevent some banking transactions with Iran, discussed later, could suggest that India is now cautious about any expansion of energy relations with Iran. Previously, the threat of imposition of U.S. sanctions had not dissuaded Indian firms from taking equity stakes in various Iranian energy projects, as shown in Table 5.

During the Bush administration, Secretary of State Rice on several occasions "expressed U.S. concern" about the pipeline deal or called it "unacceptable." Possibly contributing to India's hesitancy to move forward, the late Ambassador Richard Holbrooke, the Administration Special Representative on Pakistan and Afghanistan, during 2010 trips to Pakistan, raised the possibility that the project could be sanctioned if it is undertaken, citing enactment of CISADA. Nonetheless, energy experts in Iran12 say Iran has largely completed the pipeline extension from its network to the Pakistan border, meaning that the project could become operational if Pakistan completes construction on its side of the border, and the two are linked.

India may envision an alternative to the pipeline project, as a means of tapping into Iran's vast gas resources. During high-level economic talks in early July 2010, Iranian and Indian officials reportedly raised the issue of constructing an underwater natural gas pipeline, which would avoid going through Pakistani territory. However, such a route would presumably be much more expensive to construct than would be an overland route.

European Gas Pipeline Routes

Iran also is attempting to position itself as a gas exporter to Europe. The Obama administration, like its predecessors, takes the view that Iran be excluded from gas pipeline projects to Europe, even though the projects might make Europe less dependent on Russian gas supplies. One potential project involving Iran is the Nabucco pipeline project, which would transport Iranian gas to western Europe. Iran, Turkey, and Austria reportedly have negotiated on that project.

Another is the Trans-Adriatic Pipeline (TAP) although, as discussed below, partners in that project have announced that Iranian gas would not be involved. Iran's Energy Minister GholamHossein Nozari said on April 2, 2009, that Iran is considering negotiating a gas export route—the "Persian Pipeline"—that would send gas to Europe via Iraq, Syria, and the Mediterranean Sea.

Application to Iranian Firms or the Revolutionary Guard

Although ISA is widely understood to apply to firms around the world that reach an investment agreement with Iran, the provisions could also be applied to Iranian firms and entities subordinate to the National Iranian Oil Company (NIOC), which is supervised by the Oil Ministry. The firm that was sanctioned, Naftiran Intertrade Company (NICO), is one such entity; it is a subsidiary of NIOC. However, such entities, including Naftiran, do not do business in the United States and would not likely be harmed by any of the penalties that could be imposed under ISA. Some of the other major components of NIOC are

- The Iranian Offshore Oil Company;
- The National Iranian Gas Export Co.;
- National Iranian Tanker Company; and
- Petroleum Engineering and Development Co.

Actual construction and work is largely done through a series of contractors. Some of them, such as Khatam ol-Anbia and Oriental Kish, have been identified by the U.S. government as controlled by Iran's Islamic Revolutionary Guard Corps (IRGC) and have been sanctioned under various executive orders, discussed below.

The relationship of other Iranian contractors to the Guard, if any, is unclear. Some of the Iranian contractor firms include Pasargad Oil Co, Zagros Petrochem. Co, Sazeh Consultants, Qeshm Energy, Sadid Industrial Group, and others.

Some believe the August 2011 confirmation of Khatam ol-Anbia's chief, Rostam Ghasemi, as Oil Minister, will, over time, bolster the role of the IRGC in Iran's oil sector. Ghasemi has also taken over the chair of the Organization of Petroleum Exporting Countries (OPEC) because it is Iran's turn to hold that rotating post. Ghasemi has been subjected to asset freezes by the United States and an asset freeze and travel ban by the European Union.

However, under an agreement between OPEC andAustria, Ghasemi would be allowed to travel to Vienna (OPEC's headquarters) to attend OPEC meetings and perform his duties as rotating head of the organization.

Application to Liquefied Natural Gas

The original version of ISA did not apply to the development of liquefied natural gas.

Iran has no LNG export terminals, in part because the technology for such terminals is patented by U.S. firms and unavailable for sale to Iran. However, as noted below, CISADA specifically includes LNG in the definition of petroleum resources and therefore makes investment in LNG (or supply of LNG tankers or pipelines) sanctionable.

Table 2. Provisions and Implementation of CISADA (P.L. 111-195)

General Goals and Overview:

Expand the authorities of the Iran Sanctions Act (ISA, P.L. 104-172) to deter sales by foreign companies of gasoline to Iran. Adds new provisions sanctioning Iranians determined to be involved in human rights abuses and prohibiting transactions with foreign banks that conduct business with Revolutionary Guard and U.N.-sanctioned Iranian entities.

Statement of U.S. Policy on Sanctioning Iran's Central Bank (Bank Markazi):

Section 104 (see below) contains sense of Congress urging U.S. sanctions against Iranian Central Bank and would prohibit U.S. bank dealings with any financial institution that helps the Central Bank facilitate circumvention of U.N. resolutions on Iran.

Extension of ISA to Sales of Gasoline:

Section 102(a) contains provisions amending ISA to make sanctionable sales of gasoline and provision of services and equipment that Iran could use to manufacture its own gasoline or import gasoline. Such services include shipping or shipping insurance, and equipment (such as ships).

Sets dollar value "trigger" for such sales or services at $1 million transaction, or $5 million aggregate value (equipment or gasoline sales) in a one-year period.

Specifies that what is sanctionable includes helping Iran develop its liquefied natural gas (LNG) sector. Products whose sales is sanctionable include LNG tankers and products to build pipelines used to transport oil or LNG. Includes aviation fuel in definition of refined petroleum.

Formally reduces investment threshold to $20 million to trigger sanctionability.

Expansion of ISA Sanctions:

Section 102(b) amends ISA to add *add three sanctions to the existing menu* of six sanctions in ISA and requires the president to *impose 3 out of the 9* specified sanctions on entities determined to be violators.

(As it previously existed, ISA required the imposition of two out of six sanctions of the menu.)

U.S. Government Enforcement Mechanism:

Section 102(b) amends ISA by adding a provision similar to the House version: requiring, within 90 days of enactment (by October 1, 2010) new Federal Acquisition Regulations that mandate that firms to certify that they are not in violating of ISA as a condition of receiving a U.S. government contract, and providing for penalties for any falsification.

The Civilian Agency Acquisition Council issued the needed regulations (interim ruling) on September 29, 2010.

Paperwork that firms must sign making that certification now included as part of their contract signature package.

Additional Sanctions Against Suppliers of Nuclear, Missile, or Advanced Conventional Weapons Technology to Iran:

Section 102(a)(2) amends ISA by adding a prohibition on licensing of nuclear materials, facilities, or technology to any country which is the parent country of an entity determined to be sanctioned under ISA for providing WMD technology to Iran.

Waiver is provided on vital national security interest grounds.

Alterations to Waiver and Implementation Provisions:

Section 102(g) amends ISA to make mandatory the beginning of an investigation of potentially sanctionable activity upon receipt of credible information of a potential violation. Makes mandatory a decision on sanctionability within 180 days of the beginning of such an investigation. (Previously, 180-day period was nonbinding.)

Mandatory investigation (which goes into effect July 1, 2011) of gasoline sales to Iran can be delayed for 180 days subject to a report—by June 1, 2011—certifying that there has been a substantial reduction in gasoline sales to Iran as a result of CISADA.

Section 102(c) sets 9(c) waiver standard as "necessary to the national interest"

Section 102(g) also alters existing 4(c) ISA waiver to delay sanctions on firms of countries that are "closely cooperating" with U.S. efforts against Iran's WMD programs. (This is not an automatic "carve out" for cooperating countries.)

Section 102(g)(3) adds to ISA a "special rule" that no investigation of a potential violation need be started if a firm has ended or pledged to end its violating activity in/with Iran. "Special rule" invoked twice, as discussed above.

Required Reports:

Various reporting requirements throughout (separate from those required to trigger or justify the various sanctions or waivers).

These reporting requirements are:

- Amendment of section 10 of ISA to include a report, within 90 days of enactment, and annual thereafter, on trade between Iran and the countries of the Group of 20 Finance Ministers and Central Bank Governors. (From House version)
- Section 110 of the law (not an amendment to ISA) requires a report within 90 days, and every 180 days hence, on investments made in Iran's energy sector since January 1, 2006. The report must include significant joint ventures outside Iran in which Iranian entities are involved.
- The Section 110 report is to include an estimate of the value of ethanol imported by Iran during the reporting period.

Not clear whether Section 110 reports have been submitted to Congress.

- Section 111 (not an ISA amendment) requires a report within 90 days on the activities of export credit agencies of foreign countries in guaranteeing financing for trade with Iran).

Not clear whether report was submitted to Congress.

Expansion of ISA Definitions:

Does not include export credit agencies as a sanctionable entity under ISA (as amended). (However, a report is required on export credit agency activity, as discussed above.)

Does include LNG as petroleum resources.

As discussed in text, eliminates specific exemption of application of ISA sanctions energy sector equipment and services. This change largely mooted by November 2011 Executive Order, discussed above, which specifically sanctions sales to Iran of such equipment.

Termination Provisions:

The amendments to ISA in this law terminate if the president certifies that Iran has ceased WMD development, and has qualified for removal from the U.S. terrorism list.

However, the pre-existing version of ISA would continue to apply until the president also certifies that Iran poses no significant threat to U.S. national security, interests, or allies.

ISA Sunset:

Extends ISA sunset to December 31, 2016.

It was previously scheduled to "sunset" on December 31, 2011, as amended by the Iran Freedom Support Act (P.L. 109-293).

Additional Provisions That Are Not Amendments to ISA

Modification to U.S. Ban on Trade with and Investment in Iran:

Bans all imports of Iranian origin from the United States, with the exception of informational material. Previously, modifications to the U.S. trade ban with Iran (Executive Order 12959 of May 6, 1995) that became effective in 2000 permit imports of Iranian luxury goods, such as carpets, caviar, nuts, and dried fruits.

- Reiterates/codifies prior provisions of U.S. trade ban related to U.S. exports to Iran., which prohibit exports to Iran of all goods except food and medical devices, informational material, articles used for humanitarian assistance to Iran, or goods needed to ensure safe operation of civilian aircraft.

Contains a new section that the existing U.S. ban (by executive order) on most exports to Iran not include the exportation of services for Internet communications. Provision also states that the ban on most exports should not include goods or services needed to help nongovernmental organizations support democracy in Iran. Both provisions designed to support opposition protesters linked to Iran's "Green movement."

Implementation:

In July 2010, Treasury Office of Foreign Assets Control issued a statement that, effective September 29, 2010, the general license for imports of Iranian luxury goods will be eliminated (no such imports allowed).

This went into effect that day.

Freezing of Assets/Travel Restriction on Revolutionary Guard and Related Entities and Persons:

Mandates the president to freeze the assets of Iranian diplomats, IRGC, or other Iranian official personnel deemed a threat to U.S. national security under the International Emergency Economic Powers Act (50 USC. 1701 et seq.). Provision requires freezing of assets of families and associates of persons so designated. Also calls for a ban on travel of IRGC and affiliated persons.

Application of U.S. Trade Ban to Subsidiaries:

No provision

Mandatory Sanctions on Financial Institutions that Help Iran's Sanctioned Entities:

Section 104(c) requires the Treasury Department to develop regulations (within 90 days of enactment) to prohibit and specify penalties for any U.S. financial transactions with any foreign financial institution that

- facilitates efforts by the Revolutionary Guard to acquire WMD or fund terrorism - facilitate the activities of any person sanctioned under U.N. resolutions on Iran.
- facilitates the efforts by Iran's Central Bank to support the Guard's WMD acquisition efforts or support any U.N.
- sanctioned entity

Section 104(d) requires penalties to be specified in regulations within 90 days.

Section 104(e) requires regulations (no date specified) to make this requirement retroactive to existing accounts, pending an audit by the U.S. banks involved.

Implementation: Treasury Department regulations implementing Section 104(c) and (d) provisions issued August 16, 2010.

Regulations to implement 104(e) finalized in October 2011, based on proposals by Treasury Department's Financial Crimes Enforcement Network (FINCEN).

Sanctions on Iranian Human Rights Abusers:

Section 105 requires, within 90 days, a report listing Iranian officials (or affiliates) determined responsible for or complicit in serious human rights abuses since the June 12, 2009, Iranian election. Those listed are ineligible for a U.S. visa, their U.S. property is to be blocked, and transactions with those listed are prohibited.

On September 29, 2010, President Obama issued Executive Order 13553 providing for these sanctions. See human rights section of this paper for Iranians sanctioned.

Sanctioning Certain Information Technology Sales to Iran:

Section 106 prohibits U.S. executive agencies from contracting with firms that export sensitive technology to Iran. "Sensitive technology" is defined as hardware, software, telecommunications equipment, or other technology that restricts the free flow of information in Iran or which monitor or restrict "speech" of the people of Iran.

The contracting restriction is to be imposed "pursuant to such regulations as the president may prescribe."

The contracting regulations issued September 29, 2010, "partially" implement this requirement, with further regulations to be issued.

Treasury Department Authorization to prevent misuse of the U.S. financial system by Iran or other countries:

Section 109 authorized $102 million for FY2011 and "sums as may be necessary" for FY2012 and 2013 to the Treasury Department Office of Terrorism and Financial Intelligence. Another $100 million was authorized for FY2011 for the Financial Crimes Enforcement Network, and $113 million for FY2011 for the Bureau of Industry and Security for the Department of Commerce

Hezbollah:

Section 113 contains a sense of Congress that the president impose the full range of sanctions under the International Emergency Economic Powers Act (50 USC. 1701) on Hezbollah, and that the president renew international efforts to disarm Hezbollah in Lebanon (as called for by U.N. Security Council Resolutions 1559 and 1701).

Divestment:

Title II prevents criminal, civil, or administrative action against any investment firm or officer or adviser based on its decision to divest from securities that

- have investments or operations in Sudan described in the Sudan Accountability and Divestment Act of 2007 - or, engage in investments in Iran that would be considered sanctionable by the Senate bill.

Prevention of Transshipment, Reexportation, or Diversion of Sensitive Items to Iran:

Requires a report by the Director of National Intelligence that identifies all countries considered a concern to allow transshipment or diversion of WMD-related technology to Iran (technically: "items subject to the provision of the Export Administration Regulations").

Section 303 requires the Secretary of Commerce to designate a country as a "Destination of Possible Diversion Concern" if such country is considered to have inadequate export controls or is unwilling to prevent the diversion of U.S. technology to Iran.

Designation would set up a strict licensing requirement for U.S. exports of sensitive technologies to that country.

List of countries that are believed to be allowing diversion of specified goods or technology to Iran to be named in a report provided within 180 days of enactment.

Implementation: Not clear that the required report has been submitted.

BAN ON U.S. TRADE AND INVESTMENT WITH IRAN

A ban on U.S. trade with and investment in Iran was imposed on May 6, 1995, by President Clinton, through Executive Order 12959.[13] This followed an earlier March 1995 executive order barring U.S. investment in Iran's energy sector. The trade and investment ban was intended to blunt criticism that U.S. trade with Iran made U.S. appeals for multilateral containment of Iran less credible. Each March since 1995 (and most recently on March 10, 2010), the U.S. administration has renewed a declaration of a state of emergency that triggered the investment ban; it is likely to be renewed again in March 2011. The operation of the trade regulations is stipulated in Section 560 of the Code of Federal Regulations (Iranian Transactions Regulations, ITR's).

As noted above, in accordance with CISADA, the strict ban on imports from Iran was restored on September 29, 2010; the ban on exports to Iran was altered only slightly by CISADA.

Some modifications to the trade ban since 1999 account for the fact that trade between the United States and Iran is minimal. Total U.S.-Iran trade was about $300 million in 2010 ($208 million in exports to Iran, and $94 million in imports). Trade was about $350 million worth of goods for all of 2009 ($281 million in exports to Iran, and $67 million in imports from Iran). That is about half the value of the bilateral trade in 2008.

The following conditions and modifications, as administered by the Office of Foreign Assets Control (OFAC) of the Treasury Department, apply to the operation of the trade ban:

- Some goods related to the safe operation of civilian aircraft may be licensed for export to Iran (Section 560.528 of Title 31, C.F.R.). As recently as September 2006, the George W. Bush administration, in the interests of safe operations of civilian aircraft, permitted a sale by General Electric of Airbus engine spare partsto be installed on several Iran Air passenger aircraft (by European airline contractors). (A provision of H.R. 6296, a bill introduced in the 111th Congress, sought to prevent these sales to Iran.) An administration intent to sell Iran data to repair certain GE engines for its legacy American-made aircraft, in order to ensure safe operation, was notified to Congress on March 16, 2011. On June 23, 2011, the administration sanctioned Iran Air as a proliferation entity under Executive order 13382, rendering any future licensing of parts or repairs for Iran Air unclear.
- U.S. firms may not negotiate with Iran or to trade Iranian oil overseas, but U.S. companies may apply for licenses to conduct “swaps” of Caspian Sea oil with Iran. A Mobil Corporation application to do so was denied in April 1999, and no known applications were submitted subsequent to that first attempt.
- According to the Iranian Transactions Regulations (ITR’s), the ban does not apply to personal communications (phone calls, e-mails), or to humanitarian donations. U.S. non-governmental organizations (NGOs) require a specific license to operate in Iran, but some of these NGOs say the licensing requirements are too onerous to make work in Iran practical. For example, there are restrictions on how a U.S. NGO may expend funds in Iran, for example to hire Iranian nationals.

- Since April 1999, commercial sales of food and medical products to Iran have been allowed, on a case-by-case basis and subject to OFAC licensing. According to OFAC in April 2007, licenses for exports of medicines to treat HIV and leukemia are routinely expedited for sale to Iran, and license applications are viewed favorably for business school exchanges, earthquake safety seminars, plant and animal conservation, and medical training in Iran.
- OFAC generally declines to discuss export licenses approved, and a press account on December 24, 2010,[14] paints a picture of broad export approvals to Iran of such condiments as ice cream sprinkles, chewing gum, food additives, hot sauces, body-building supplements, and other goods that appear to have uses other than those that are purely humanitarian or nutritive. U.S. exporters widely mentioned include Mars Co. (candy manufacturer); Kraft Foods; Wrigley's (gum); and McCormick and Co. (spices). Some goods were sold through a Revolutionary Guard-owned chains of stores in Iran called Qods; as well as a government owned Shahrvand store and a chain called Refah. OFAC officials indicated in the press accounts that such licenses were not in contradiction with U.S. law or policy, although there might have been less than full scrutiny of some Iranian end users and that such scrutiny might be increased in future licensing decisions.
- As far as financing of approved U.S. sales to Iran, private letters of credit can be used to finance approved transactions, but no U.S. government credit guarantees are available, and U.S. exporters are not permitted to deal directly with Iranian banks. The FY2001 agriculture appropriations law (P.L. 106-387) contained a provision banning the use of official credit guarantees for food and medical salesto Iran and other countries on the U.S. terrorism list, except Cuba, although allowing for a presidential waiver to permit such credit guarantees. No U.S. administration has authorized credit guarantees, to date. In December 2004, the trade ban was further modified to allow Americans to freely engage in ordinary publishing activities with entities in Iran (and Cuba and Sudan).
- In April 2000, the trade ban was further eased to allow U.S. importation of Iranian nuts, dried fruits, carpets, and caviar. Financing was permitted for U.S. importers of these goods. The United States was the largest market for Iranian carpets before the 1979 revolution, but U.S. anti-dumping tariffs imposed on Iranian products in 1986

dampened of many Iranian products. As discussed above, CISADA ended approval of such imports as of October 1, 2010. Prior to the entry into force of this CISADA provision, the number one U.S. import from Iran was pomegranate juice concentrate. Iranian carpets were another popular import, despite a U.S. tariff of about 3%-6%. Imports of Iranian caviar carried a duty of about 15%.

Non-Application to Foreign Refined Oil with Iranian Content

The ban on trade with Iran operates largely on items produced in and originating from Iran itself. In the case of crude oil, the United States, as noted, cannot import or trade overseas any Iranian crude oil.

However, existing regulations do not ban the importation, from foreign refiners, of gasoline or other energy products in which Iranian oil is contained and mixed with oil from other producers. The rationale for the regulation is that the product of a specific refinery is considered a product of the country where that refinery is located, and not a product of Iran, even if the product has some Iran-origin content. Some experts say that it is feasible to exclude Iranian content from any refinery, if there were a decision to ban U.S. imports of products with any Iranian content at all.

Non-Application to Foreign Subsidiaries of U.S. Firms

The U.S. trade ban does not bar subsidiaries of U.S. firms from dealing with Iran, as long as the subsidiary has no operational relationship to the parent company. For legal and policy purposes, foreign subsidiaries are considered foreign persons, not U.S. persons, and are subject to the laws of the country in which the subsidiaries are incorporated. The March 7, 2010, *New York Times* article, cited above, discusses some subsidiaries of U.S. firms that have been active in Iran and which have also received U.S. government contracts, grants, loans, or loan guarantees. Among major foreign subsidiaries of U.S. firms that have traded with Iran are the following:

- U.S. energy equipment firms. Some subsidiaries of such firms may still be in the Iranian market, according to their "10-K" filings with the Securities and Exchange Commission. These include Natco Group,[15] Overseas Shipholding Group,[16] UOP (United Oil Products, a

Honeywell subsidiary based in Britain),[17] Itron[18], Fluor,[19] Flowserve,[20] Parker Drilling, Vantage Energy Services,[21] Weatherford,[22] and a few others. UOP reportedly sells refinery gear to Iran; new sales of which may be sanctionable under ISA, as amended by CISADA. In September 2011, the Commerce Department fined Flowserve $2.5 million to settle 288 charges of unlicensed exports and re-exports of oil industry equipment to Iran, Syria, and other countries.

- An Irish subsidiary of the Coca Cola company provides syrup for the U.S.-brand soft drink to an Iranian distributor, Khoshgovar. Local versions of both Coke and of Pepsi (with Iranian-made syrups) are also marketed in Iran by distributors who licensed the recipes for those soft drinks before the Islamic revolution and before the trade ban was imposed on Iran.
- Transammonia Corp., via a Swiss-based subsidiary, is said to be conducting business with Iran to help it export ammonia, a growth export for Iran.
- Press reports in early October 2011 indicated that subsidiaries of Kansas-based Koch Industries may have sold equipment to Iran to be used in petrochemical plants (making methanol) and possibly oil refineries, among other equipment. However, the reports say the sales ended as of 2007, a time at which foreign firm sales of refinery equipment to Iran were not clearly sanctionable under ISA. [23]

Subsidiaries Exiting Iran

As international sanctions against Iran have increased in recent years, many foreign subsidiaries have decided that the risks of continuing to do business with Iran outweigh the benefits. These decisions to leave the Iran market might have been reached in discussions with their U.S. parent corporations.

- Chemical manufacturer Huntsman announced in January 2010 its subsidiaries would halt sales to Iran.
- Halliburton. On January 11, 2005, Iran said it had contracted with U.S. company Halliburton, and an Iranian company, Oriental Kish, to drill for gas in Phases 9 and 10 of South Pars. Halliburton reportedly provided $30 million to $35 million worth of services per year through Oriental Kish, leaving unclear whether Halliburton would be considered in violation of the U.S. trade and investment ban or the

Iran Sanctions Act (ISA),[24] because the deals involved a subsidiary ofHalliburton (Cayman Islands-registered Halliburton Products and Service, Ltd., based in Dubai). On April 10, 2007, Halliburton announced that its subsidiaries were no longer operating in Iran, as promised in January 2005.

- General Electric (GE). The firm announced in February 2005 that it would seek no new business in Iran, and it reportedly wound down preexisting contracts by July 2008. GE was selling Iran equipment and services for hydroelectric, oil and gas services, and medical diagnostic projects through Italian, Canadian, and French subsidiaries.
- Oilfield services firm Smith International said on March 1, 2010, it would stop sales to Iran by its subsidiaries.
- On March 1, 2010, Caterpillar Corp. said it had altered its policies to prevent foreign subsidiaries from selling equipment to independent dealers that have been reselling the equipment to Iran.[25] Ingersoll Rand, maker of air compressors and cooling systems, followed suit.[26]
- In April 2010, it was reported that foreign partners of several U.S. or other multinational accounting firms had cut their ties with Iran, including KPMG of the Netherlands, and local affiliates of U.S. firms PricewaterhouseCoopers and Ernst and Young.[27]
- In the 110th Congress, S. 970, S. 3227, S. 3445, and three House-passed bills (H.R. 1400, H.R. 7112, and H.R. 957) - would have applied sanctions to the parent companies of U.S. subsidiaries if those subsidiaries are directed by the parent company to trade with Iran. The Senate version of CISADA contained a similar provision, but it was taken out in conference action. A provision of H.R. 6296, the bill introduced in the 111th Congress, would apply this sanction. Provisions in the 112th Congress are discussed at the section below on pending legislation.

BANKING: TREASURY DEPARTMENT FINANCIAL MEASURES, CISADA, AND PATRIOT ACT SECTION 311

U.S. efforts to shut Iran out of the international banking system have gained strength as other countries have joined the effort. These efforts have been implemented by the Treasury Department through “targeted financial measures," and several other actions, including designation of Iranian entities as violators of various Executive Orders.

During 2006-2010, strengthened by leverage provided in five U.N. Security Council Resolutions, then Undersecretary of the Treasury Stuart Levey and his aides convinced at least 80 foreign banks that dealing with Iran entails financial risk and furthers terrorism and proliferation. Treasury Secretary Timothy Geithner has described Levey as having "led the design of aremarkably successful program"[28] with regard to targeting Iran's proliferation networks. Levey left office in April 2011 and was replaced by Daniel Cohen. These actions followed efforts to prevent Iran from accessing the U.S. financial system.

On September 6, 2006, the Treasury Department barred U.S. banks from handling any indirect transactions ("U-turn transactions," meaning transactions with non-Iranian foreign banks that are handling transactions on behalf of an Iranian bank) with Iran's Bank Saderat, which the administration accused of providing funds to Hezbollah.[29] Bank Sepah is subject to asset freezes and transactions limitations as a result of Resolutions 1737 and 1747. The Treasury Department extended that U-Turn restriction to all Iranian banks on November 6, 2008.

The Treasury Department has also used punishments to pressure firms to cease doing business with Iran. In 2004, the Treasury Department fined UBS $100 million for the unauthorized movement of U.S. dollars to Iran and other sanctioned countries, and in December 2005, the Treasury Department fined Dutch bank ABN Amro $80 million for failing to fully report the processing of financial transactions involving Iran's Bank Melli (and another bank partially owned by Libya). In the biggest such instance, on December 16, 2009, the Treasury Department announced that Credit Suisse would pay a $536 million settlement to the United States for illicitly processing Iranian transactions with U.S. banks. Credit Suisse, according to the Treasury Department, saw business opportunity by picking up the transactions business from a competitor who had, in accordance with U.S. regulations discussed below, ceased processing dollar transactions for Iranian banks. Credit Suisse also pledged to cease doing business with Iran.

On December 17, 2008, the U.S. Attorney for the Southern District of New York filed a civil action seeking to seize the assets of the Assa Company, a UK-chartered entity.

Assa allegedly was maintaining the interests of Bank Melli in an office building in New York City. An Iranian foundation, the Alavi Foundation, allegedly is an investor in the building.

Banking Provisions of CISADA

The Treasury Department efforts have been enhanced substantially by the authorities of Section 104 of CISADA and U.N. and EU sanctions. Broadly, Section 104 of CISADA seeks to exclude foreign banks from operating in the United States if these banks conduct transactions with the Revolutionary Guard or its affiliates, or with Iranian entities that are subject to international or U.S. sanctions (under various Executive Orders issued under IEEPA, such as 13224 and 13382 discussed below).

The premise of the provision is that cutting off Iran's access to the international financial system would make it more difficult for Iran to move its money.

The binding provisions of Section 104 of CISADA require the Secretary of the Treasury to prescribe several sets of regulations to forbid U.S. banks from opening new "correspondent accounts" or "payable through accounts"— or force the cancellation of existing such accounts— with foreign banks that process "significant transactions" with the entities discussed above. Foreign banks that do not have operations in the United States typically establish such accounts with U.S. banks as a means of accessing the U.S. financial system and financial industry. The entities with which transactions would trigger the sanctions are:

- The Islamic Revolutionary Guard Corps (IRGC) or any of its agents or affiliates that are sanctioned under U.S. executive orders. The two executive orders that have served as the principal source of U.S. sanctions against Iranian firms and organizations are Executive Order 13224 (September 23, 2001) and 13382 (June 28, 2005), discussed elsewhere in this paper.
- Any entity that is sanctioned by U.S. executive orders such as the two mentioned above. To date, over 125 entities (including individuals), almost all of them Iran-based or of Iranian origin, have been designated for Iran-related proliferation or terrorism activities under these orders.
  A full list is at the end of this paper.
- Any entity designated under the various U.N. Security Council resolutions adopted to impose sanctions on Iran.
- Any entity that assists Iran's Central Bank in efforts to help the IRGC acquire weapons of mass destruction or support international terrorism.

Sanctions

As of October 13, 2011, the United States has not announced any sanctions against any bank under this provision of CISADA.

Section 311 of the Patriot Act

On November 21, 2011, the administration took further steps to isolate Iran's banking system and to dissuade foreign banks and countries from dealing with any Iranian bank. Secretary of Treasury Geithner announced that day that the administration had acted under Section 311 of the USA Patriot Act (31 USC. 5318A) to identify Iran as a "jurisdiction of primary money laundering concern[30]—that its financial system, including the Central Bank, constitutes a threat to governments or financial institutions that do business with these banks. Banks that do business with the Iranian financial system were declared at risk of supporting Iran's pursuit of nuclear weapons, its support for terrorism, and its efforts to deceive financial institutions and evade sanctions. The designation carried no immediate penalty, per se, but it imposes additional requirements on U.S. banks to ensure against improper Iranian access to the U.S. financial system. It also likely has the effect of causing foreign banks to hesitate to do business with Iran.

TERRORISM LIST DESIGNATION-RELATED SANCTIONS

Several U.S. sanctions are in effect as a result of Iran's presence on the U.S. "terrorism list." The list was established by Section 6(j) of the Export Administration Act of 1979 (P.L. 96-72, as amended), sanctioning countries determined to have provided repeated support for acts of international terrorism.

Iran was added to the list in January 1984, following the October 1983 bombing of the U.S. Marine barracks in Lebanon (believed perpetrated by Hezbollah). Sanctions imposed as a consequence include a ban on U.S. foreign aid to Iran; restrictions on U.S. exports to Iran of dual use items; and requires the United States to vote against international loans to Iran.

- The terrorism list designation restricts sales of U.S. dual use items (Export Administration Act, as continued through presidential authorities under the International Emergency Economic Powers Act, IEEPA, as implemented by executive orders), and, under other laws, bans direct U.S. financial assistance (Section 620A of the Foreign Assistance Act, FAA, P.L. 87-195) and arms sales (Section 40 of the Arms Export Control Act, P.L. 95-92, as amended), and requires the United States to vote to oppose multilateral lending to the designated countries (Section 327 of the Anti-Terrorism and Effective Death Penalty Act of 1996, P.L. 104-132). Waivers are provided under these laws, but successive foreign aid appropriations laws since the late 1980s ban direct assistance to Iran (loans, credits, insurance, Ex-Im Bank credits) without providing for a waiver.

- Section 307 of the FAA (added in 1985) names Iran as unable to benefit from U.S. contributions to international organizations, and require proportionate cuts if these institutions work in Iran. No waiver is provided for.
- The Anti-Terrorism and Effective Death Penalty Act (Sections 325 and 326 of P.L. 104-132) requires the president to withhold U.S. foreign assistance to any country that provides to a terrorism list country foreign assistance or arms. Waivers are provided.

U.S. sanctions laws do not bar disaster aid. The United States donated $125,000, through relief agencies, to help victims of two earthquakes in Iran (February and May 1997), and another $350,000 worth of aid to the victims of a June 22, 2002, earthquake. (The World Bank provided some earthquake related lending as well.)

The United States provided $5.7 million in assistance (out of total governmental pledges of about $32 million, of which $17 million have been remitted) to the victims of the December 2003 earthquake in Bam, Iran, which killed as many as 40,000 people and destroyed 90% of Bam's buildings.

The United States military flew in 68,000 kilograms of supplies to Bam. In the Bam case, there was also a temporary exemption made in the regulations to allow for a general licensing (no need for a specific license) for donations to Iran of humanitarian goods by American citizens and organizations.

Those exemptions were extended several times but expired in March 2004. When that expiration occurred, the policy reverted to a requirement for specific licensing (application to OFAC) and approval process for donations and operations in Iran of U.S.-based humanitarian NGO's.

Executive Order 13224

The separate, but related, Executive Order 13324 (September 23, 2001) authorizes the president to freeze the assets of and bar U.S. transactions with entities determined to be supporting international terrorism. This order, issued two weeks after the September 11 attacks, under the authority of the IEEPA, the National Emergencies Act, the U.N. Participation Act of 1945, and Section 301 of the U.S. Code, was intended to primarily target Al Qaeda-related entities. However, it has increasingly been applied to Iranian entities. Such Iran-related entities named and sanctioned under this order are in *Table 6*, which also contains the names of Iranian entities sanctioned under other orders and under United Nations resolutions. On October 12, 2011, the Treasury Department designated Mahan Air, an airline operating in Iran and the Persian Gulf region, under this Order, for allegedly helping the Qods Force (the arm of Iran's Revolutionary Guard that supports pro-Iranian movements abroad) ship weapons and other gear. The announcement followed U.S. revelations of an alleged Qods plot to assassinate the Saudi Ambassador to the United States in Washington, D.C. – the Qods officers and others allegedly involved in this purported plot were sanctioned under this Order the previous day (October 11). On July 28, 2011, the Treasury Department designated six members of Al Qaeda under this order for allegedly serving as financiers for Al Qaeda. The six are based in Iran, according to the Treasury Department and are allowed to operate from Iran under an agreement between Al Qaeda and the Iranian government.

PROLIFERATION-RELATED U.S. SANCTIONS

Iran is prevented from receiving advanced technology from the United States under relevant and Iran-specific anti-proliferation laws[31] and by Executive Order 13382 (June 28, 2005). Some of these laws and executive measures seek to penalize foreign firms and countries that provide equipment to Iran's WMD programs.

Iran-Iraq Arms Nonproliferation Act

The Iran-Iraq Arms Nonproliferation Act (P.L. 102-484) imposes a number of sanctions on foreign entities that supply Iran with WMD technology or "destabilizing numbers and types of conventional weapons." Sanctions imposed on violating entities include a ban, for two years, on U.S. government procurement from that entity, and a two-year ban on licensing U.S. exports to that entity. A sanction to ban imports to the United States from the entity is authorized.

If the violator is determined to be a foreign country, sanctions to be imposed are a one-year ban on U.S. assistance to that country; a one-year requirement that the United States vote against international lending to it; a one-year suspension of U.S. co-production agreements with the country; a one-year suspension of technical exchanges with the country in military or dual use technology; and a one-year ban on sales of U.S. arms to the country. The president is also authorized to deny the country most-favored-nation trade status; and to impose a ban on U.S. trade with the country.

The Iran-Iraq Arms Nonproliferation Act (Section 1603) also provides for a "presumption of denial" for all dual use exports to Iran (which would include computer software). A waiver to permit such exports, on a case-by-case basis, is provided for.

Iran-North Korea-Syria Nonproliferation Act

The Iran Nonproliferation Act (P.L. 106-178), now called the Iran-North Korea-Syria Non-Proliferation Act (INKSNA) authorizes sanctions on foreign *persons* (individuals or corporations, not countries or governments) that are determined by the administration to have assisted Iran's WMD programs. It bans U.S. extraordinary payments to the Russian Aviation and Space Agency in connection with the international space station unless the president can certify that the agency or entities under its control had not transferred any WMD or missile technology to Iran within the year prior.[32] (A Continuing Resolution for FY2009, which funded the U.S. government through March 2009, waived this law to allow NASA to continue to use Russian vehicles to access the International Space Station.) Pending legislation in the 112th Congress, discussed later, would amend INKSNA.

Executive Order 13382

Executive Order 13382 (June 28, 2005) allows the president to block the assets of proliferators of weapons of mass destruction (WMD) and their supporters under the authority granted by the International Emergency Economic Powers Act (IEEPA, 50 USC. 1701 et seq.), the National Emergencies Act (50 USC. 1601 et seq.), and Section 301 of Title 3, United States Code.

Table 6 lists Iran-related entities sanctioned under the order. As an example, the IRGC is named as a proliferation entity under E.O. 13382.

Foreign Aid Restrictions for Suppliers of Iran

In addition, successive foreign aid appropriations punish the Russian Federation for assisting Iran by withholding 60% of any U.S. assistance to the Russian Federation unless it terminates technical assistance to Iran's nuclear and ballistic missiles programs.

U.S. Efforts to Promote Divestment

A growing trend not only in Congress but in several states is to require or call for or require divestment of shares of firms that have invested in Iran's energy sector (at the same levels considered sanctionable under the Iran Sanctions Act).[33] The concept of these sanctions is to express the view of Western and other democracies that Iran is an outcast internationally.

Legislation in the 110th Congress, H.R. 1400, did not require divestment, but would have required a presidential report on firms that have invested in Iran's energy sector. Another bill, H.R. 1357, required government pension funds to divest of shares in firms that have made ISA-sanctionable investments in Iran's energy sector and bar government and private pension funds from future investments in such firms. Two other bills, H.R. 2347 (passed by the House on July 31, 2007) and S. 1430, would protect mutual fund and other investment companies from shareholder action for any losses that would occur from divesting in firms that have investing in Iran's energy sector.

In the 111th Congress, H.R. 1327 (Iran Sanctions Enabling Act), a bill similar to H.R. 2347 of the 110th Congress, was reported by the Financial Services Committee on April 28, 2009. It passed the House on October 14, 2009, by a vote of 414-6. A similar bill. S. 1065, was introduced in the Senate. Provisions along these lines was contained in CISADA (P.L. 111-195)—in particular providing a "safe harbor" for investment managers who sell shares of firms that invest in Iran's energy sector.

U.S. Sanctions Intended to Support Democratic Change in Iran or Alter Iran's Foreign Policy

A trend since the June 2009 Iran election dispute has been to promote the prospects for the domestic opposition in Iran. Proposals to target the Revolutionary Guard for sanctions, discussed throughout, represent one facet of that trend. The IRGC is involved in Iran's WMD programs but it is also the key instrument through which the regime has suppressed the pro-democracy movement. Several measures to support the opposition's ability to communicate, to reduce the regime's ability to monitor or censor Internet communications and to identify and sanction Iranian human rights abusers, were included in CISADA.

Earlier legislation, the Iran Freedom Support Act (IFSA, P.L. 109-293), represented a congressional effort to promote the prospects for opponents of the regime. That law authorized "sums as may be necessary" to assist Iranians who are "dedicated" to "democratic values ... and the adoption of a democratic form of government in Iran"; and "advocates the adherence by Iran to nonproliferation regimes...."

Expanding Internet and Communications Freedoms

Some Members have focused on expanding Internet freedom in Iran or preventing the Iranian government from using the Internet to identify opponents. Subtitle D of the FY2010 Defense Authorization Act (P.L. 111-84), called the "VOICE" (Victims of Iranian Censorship) Act contained several provisions to increase U.S. broadcasting to Iran and to identify (in a report to be submitted 180 days after enactment, or April 25, 2009) companies that are selling Iran technology equipment that it can use to suppress or monitor the internet usage of Iranians. The Act authorized funds to document Iranian human rights abuses since the June 12, 2009, presidential election. Another provision (Section 1241) required an administration report, not later than January 31, 2010, on U.S. enforcement of sanctions against Iran, and the effect of those sanctions on Iran.

In the 111th Congress, the "Reduce Iranian Cyber-Suppression Act," (S. 1475 and H.R. 3284) was incorporated into CISADA. It authorizes the president to ban U.S. government contracts with foreign companies that sell technology that Iran could use to monitor or control Iranian usage of the internet. Another provision of CISADA (Section 103(b)(2)) exempts from the U.S. export ban on Iran equipment to help Iranians communicate and use the Internet. The provisions were directed, in part, against firms, including a joint venture between Nokia (Finland) and Siemens (Germany), reportedly sold Internet monitoring and censorship technology to Iran in 2008.[34] Perhaps to avoid further embarrassment, Siemens announced on January 27, 2010, that it would stop signing new business deals in Iran as of mid-2010.[35] There is some concern that a large Chinese firm, Huawei, might have sold Iran Internet monitoring or censorship gear as part of its work in Iran's communications industry although there is no clear information that it has done so.

In line with this trend, on March 8, 2010, OFAC amended the Iran Transactions Regulations that implement the U.S.-Iran trade ban to provide for a general license for providing to Iranians free mass market software in order to facilitate internet communications. The ruling appeared to incorporate the major features of a proposal in the 111th Congress, H.R. 4301, the "Iran Digital Empowerment Act." The OFAC determination required a waiver of the provision of the Iran-Iraq Arms Nonproliferation Act (Section 1606 waiver provision) discussed above.

To counter some of the efforts above, and among other measures, in 2011 the Iranian government established a "cyber police" force. Part of the force's duties are to sensitize young Iranians to the government view that Western countries are using the Internet to undermine Iran's Islamic values and government.[36]

Measures to Sanction Human Rights Abuses and Promote the Opposition

Another part of the effort to help Iran's opposition has been legislation to sanction regime officials involved in suppressing the domestic opposition in Iran. Senator John McCain proposed to offer amendments to S. 2799 (the Senate version of what became H.R. 2194) to focus on banning travel and freezing assets of those Iranians determined to be human rights abusers. These provisions were included in the conference report on CISADA. The provisions were similar to those of Senator McCain's earlier stand alone bill, S. 3022, the "Iran Human Rights Sanctions Act." Companion measures in the House were H.R. 4647 and H.R. 4649.

On September 29, 2010, the administration implemented the CISADA provision when President Obama signed an Executive Order (13553) providing for the CISADA sanctions against Iranians determined to be responsible for or complicit in post-2009 Iran election human rights abuses. Along with the order, an initial group of eight Iranian officials were penalized, including Mohammad Ali Jafari, the commander-in-chief of the IRGC, and several other officials who were in key security or judicial positions at the time of the June 2009 election and aftermath. Several additional officials and security force entities have been sanctioned under the Order since, as shown in the table at the end of this paper. Under State Department interpretations of the executive order, if an entity is designated, all members of that entity are ineligible for visas to enter the United States.[37]

Similar sanctions against many of these same officials—as well as several others—have been imposed by the European Union - a total of 61 Iranians have been so sanctioned by the EU to date, including 29 Iranian officials sanctioned on October 5, 2011.

Executive Order 13438 and 13572: Sanctioning Iranian Involvement in the Region

Some sanctions have been imposed to try to punish Iran's involvement in certain activities in the region. On July 7, 2007, President Bush issued Executive Order 13438. The order sanctions Iranian persons who are posing a threat to Iraqi stability, presumably by providing arms or funds to Shiite militias there. Some persons sanctioned have been Qods Force officers, some have been Iraqi Shiite militia-linked figures, and some entities have been sanctioned as well.

More recently, the Qods Force and a number of Iranian Qods Force officers, including Qods Force commander Qasem Soleimani, have been sanctioned under Executive Order 13572. That order was issued on April 29, 2011, targeting Syrian officials and other responsible for human rights abuses and repression of the Syrian people.

The Iranians were sanctioned for allegedly helping Syria commit abuses against protesters and repress its domestic opposition movement that has conducted nationwide demonstration since March 2011. In September 2011, the European Union similarly sanctioned the Qods Force for its purported assistance to Syria's repression.

Separate Visa Ban

On July 8, 2011, in conjunction with Britain, the United States imposed visa restrictions on more than 50 Iranian officials for participating in political repression in Iran.

The State Department announcement stated that the names of those subject to the ban would not be released because visa records are confidential. The action was taken under the authorities of Section 212(a)(3)(C) of the Immigration and Nationality Act, which renders inadmissible to the United States a foreign person whose activities could have serious consequences for the United States.

Blocked Iranian Property and Assets

Iranian leaders continue to assert that the United States is holding Iranian assets, and that this is an impediment to improved relations. A U.S.-Iran Claims Tribunal at the Hague continues to arbitrate cases resulting from the 1980 break in relations and freezing of some of Iran's assets. Major cases yet to be decided center on hundreds of Foreign Military Sales (FMS) cases between the United States and the Shah's regime, which Iran claims it paid for but were unfulfilled. About $400 million in proceeds from the resale of that equipment was placed in a DOD FMS account an remains in this escrow account. Additionally, according to the Treasury Department "Terrorist Assets Report" for 2010, about $48 million in Iranian diplomatic property and accounts remains blocked - this amount includes proceeds from rents received on the former Iranian embassy in Washington, D.C. and ten other properties in several states, along with six related bank accounts.[38]

Other past disputes include the mistaken U.S. shoot-down on July 3, 1988, of an Iranian Airbus passenger jet (Iran Air flight 655), for which the United States, in accordance with an ICJ judgment, paid Iran $61.8 million in compensation ($300,000 per wage earning victim, $150,000 per nonwage earner) for the 248 Iranians killed. The United States has not compensated Iran for the airplane itself. As it has in past similar cases, the Bush administration opposed a terrorism lawsuit against Iran by victims of the U.S. Embassy Tehran seizure on the grounds of diplomatic obligation.[39]

U.N. Sanctions

The U.S. sanctions discussed in this report are more extensive than those imposed, to date, by the United Nations Security Council or by individual foreign countries or groups of countries, such as the European Union.

However, U.N. sanctions apply to all U.N. member states, and therefore tend to be more effective than unilateral sanctions. There is increasing convergence among all these varying sets of sanctions.

As part of a multilateral process of attempting to convince Iran to choose the path of negotiations or face further penalty, during 2006-2008, three U.N. Security Council resolutions—1737, 1747, and 1803—imposed sanctions primarily on Iran's weapons of mass destruction (WMD) infrastructure. The multilateral group negotiation with Iran ("P5+1:" the Security Council permanent members, plus Germany) at the same time offered Iran incentives to suspend uranium enrichment. After failed negotiations with Iran during 2009, Resolution 1929 was adopted on June 9, 2010, by a vote of 12-2 (Turkey and Brazil), with one abstention (Lebanon). (Iranian entities and persons sanctioned by the United Nations are in *Table 6*.)

The main points of Resolution 1929 are:[40]

- It adds several firms affiliated with the Revolutionary Guard firms to the list of sanctioned entities.
- It makes mandatory a ban on travel for Iranian persons named in it and in previous resolutions—including those Iranians for whom there was a nonbinding travel ban in previous resolutions.
- It gives countries the authorization to inspect any shipments—and to dispose of its cargo—if the shipments are suspected to carry contraband items. However, inspections on the high seas are subject to concurrence by the country that owns that ship. This provision is modeled after a similar provision imposed on North Korea, which did cause that country to reverse some of its shipments.
- It prohibits countries from allowing Iran to invest in uranium mining and related nuclear technologies, or nuclear-capable ballistic missile technology.
- It bans sales to Iran of most categories of heavy arms to Iran and requests restraint in sales of light arms, but does not bar sales of missiles not on the "U.N. Registry of Conventional Arms."
- It requires countries to insist that their companies refrain from doing business with Iran *if* there is reason to believe that such business could further Iran's WMD programs.
- It requests, but does not mandate, that countries prohibit Iranian banks to open in their countries, or for their banks to open in Iran, *if* doing so could contribute to Iran's WMD activities.

- It authorizes the establishment of a "panel of experts," which is chaired by senior State Department arms control and proliferation adviser Robert Einhorn, to assist the U.N. sanctions committee in implementing the Resolution and previous Iran resolutions, and to suggest ways of more effective implementation.
- The resolution did not make mandatory some measures that reportedly were considered, including barring any foreign investment in Iranian bond offerings; banning insurance for transport contracts for shipments involving Iran; banning international investment in Iran's energy sector; banning the provision of trade credits to Iran, or banning all financial dealings with Iranian banks.

Table 3. Summary of Provisions of U.N. Resolutions on Iran Nuclear Program (1737, 1747, 1803, and 1929)

Require Iran to suspend uranium enrichment, and to refrain from any development of ballistic missiles that are nuclear capable (1929). Prohibit transfer to Iran of nuclear, missile, and dual use items to Iran, except for use in light-water reactors Prohibit Iran from exporting arms or WMD-useful technology. Prohibit Iran from investing abroad in uranium mining, related nuclear technologies or nuclear capable ballistic missile technology. Freeze the assets of over 80 named Iranian persons and entities, including Bank Sepah, and several corporate affiliates of the Revolutionary Guard. Require that countries ban the travel of over 40 named Iranians Mandates that countries not export major combat systems to Iran. Calls for "vigilance" (a nonbinding call to cut off business) with respect to all Iranian banks, particularly Bank Melli and Bank Saderat. Calls for vigilance (voluntary restraint) with respect to providing international lending to Iran and providing trade credits and other financing and financial interactions.

Calls on countries to inspect cargoes carried by Iran Air Cargo and Islamic Republic of Iran Shipping Lines—or by any ships in national or international waters—if there are indications they carry cargo banned for carriage to Iran.

Searches in international waters would require concurrence of the country where the ship is registered.

A Sanctions Committee, composed of the 15 members of the Security Council, monitors Implementation of all Iran sanctions and collects and disseminates information on Iranian violations and other entities involved in banned activities.

A "panel of experts" is empowered by 1929 to make recommendations for improved enforcement.

Source: Text of U.N. Security Council resolutions 1737, 1747, 1803, and 1929. http://www.un.org. More information on specific provisions of each of these resolutions and the nuclear negotiations with Iran is in CRS Report. CRS Report RL32048, Iran: U.S. Concerns and Policy Responses, by Kenneth Katzman.

INTERNATIONAL IMPLEMENTATION AND COMPLIANCE

U.S. allies have generally supported and joined the Obama administration's sanctions toward Iran, in part because the approach is perceived as not purely punitive, and in part because their own concerns about Iran's nuclear advancement have increased. U.S. and European/allied approaches have been gradually converging since 2002, when the nuclear issue came to the fore, but as of 2010, an unprecedented degree of global consensus has emerged on how to deal with Iran.

There is a degree of consensus among experts that many countries, not only allies of the United States, are complying with the provisions of U.N. sanctions, but there are selected exceptions (discussed below). Implementation appears to be somewhat less complete in Iran's immediate region, perhaps because its neighbors do not want confrontation with Iran and are hesitant to disrupt traditional relationships among traders and businessmen in the region.

European Union and Other Western States

In its July 27, 2010, sanctions measures, the product of consensus among the EU states, the EU countries imposed sanctions on Iran that exceed those mandated in Security Council resolutions. Concurrent with the EU announcement, not only Norway (not an EU member) but also Canada and Australia announced similar, although less sweeping, Iran sanctions. A comparison between U.S., U.N., and EU sanctions against Iran is contained in the chart below, although noting that there are differing legal bases and authorities for these sanctions. A U.S. president cannot mandate a foreign company take any particular action; however, the U.S. government can penalize or reward foreign firms who take action that supports U.S. objectives. U.N. Security Council resolutions are considered binding on U.N. member states. The EU clarified in late October 2010, that its sanctions against Iran do not ban importation of Iranian oil and gas, nor do they ban exports of gasoline to Iran.

Sacking of British Embassy in Tehran and Subsequent Action

On November 21, 2011, in a concerted action with those taken by the U.S. Treasury Department (see above under Section 311 of the Patriot Act), Britain and Canada announced they would no longer do business with Iran's financial institutions. Iran's parliament subsequently voted to downgrade relations with Britain, a move that, on November 29, 2011, contributed to the overrunning of the British Embassy in Tehran by pro-government students, with at least the partial apparent complicity of regime security forces. That attack prompted Britain to give all Iranian diplomats 48 hours to leave Britain, and precipitated a European Union meeting on December 1, 2011.

At that meeting, the EU states:

- Designated an additional 180 Iranian entities, mostly those linked to the Revolutionary Guard, as subject to assets freezes and travel bans. One of the entities is the Islamic Republic of Iran Shipping Lines (IRISL).
- Discussed, but did not agree to, a French proposal that EU member states voluntarily cease purchases of Iranian crude oil. Opposition from economically-troubled Greece, which imports a substantial portion of its oil from Iran, reportedly caused the proposal to be tabled until a ministerial meeting in a few weeks. By that time, it is believed Greece might be able to line up new oil suppliers.

Japan and South Korea

In early September 2010, Japan and then South Korea announced Iran sanctions similar to those of the EU. Both countries adopted measures limiting trade financing for Iran, limiting new banking relations with Iran, sanctioning numerous named Iranian entities, and restricting new projects in Iran's energy sector. The sanctions adopted by both were far more extensive than was expected by U.S. officials. At the same time, Japan and South Korea are said to fear moves by the United States and the EU to sanction Iran's Central Bank or promote a voluntary halt to purchases of Iranian oil – both get substantial oil volumes from Iran.

India

India has generally been considered friendly toward Iran and unlikely to impose any national sanctions on that country. Therefore, many experts were surprised when India's central bank, in late December 2010, announced that it would no longer use a regional body, the Asian Clearing Union, to handle transactions with Iran. The Asian Clearing Union, based in Tehran, was set up in the 1970s by the United Nations to ease commerce among Asian nations. There have been allegations in recent years that Iran might be using the Clearing Union to handle transactions so as to avoid limitations imposed by European and other banks.

The Indian move complicated India's purchases of about 350,000-400,000 barrels per day of Iranian oil, and Indian officials subsequently undertook negotiations with Iran to find an alternate mechanism to clear Indian payments for that oil and other Iranian goods. Still, the Indian move— and the reported difficulty in agreeing to a replacement payments mechanism—appeared to signal that India was taking steps to join U.S./European-led efforts to shut Iran out of the international financial system. The Indian move followed President Obama's visit there in November 2010.

Several banks considered as replacement mechanisms were either under U.N. sanctions or fear fallout (restrictions in the U.S. banking system) from transacting banking business for Iran. In February 2011, India and Iran agreed to use an Iranian bank, Europaisch-Iranische Handelsbank (EIH) to clear the payments. EIH has accounts with National Iranian Oil Company as well as with the Central Bank of Germany, rendering the bank able to process the Indian payments to Iran. Some Members of Congress had characterized that bank as one of Iran's few remaining access points to the European financial system and had asked the German government to order it closed.[41] On May 23, 2011, the EU named EIH and about 100 other entities as Iran proliferation-related activities, rendering India and Iran again in search of an alternative payments mechanism. With approximately $6.3 billion in oil payments due Iran building up in an escrow account, in July 2011 Iran threatened to reduce or cut off entirely oil shipments to India. In late July 2011, the two identified Turkey's Halkbank as at least an interim solution, and about $1.3 billion was transferred to Iran. Iranian officials said that about $5 billion was still due, although on September 4, 2011, Iran's Central Bank Governor said India had fully settled its debt. Perhaps because of the payments difficulties, some Indian firms, including Reliance Industries, Ltd, have reduced their crude oil purchases from Iran.

Separately, the majority owner of EIH, Iran's Bank of Industry and Mines (BIM), was sanctioned by the United States as a proliferation entity under Executive Order 13382, for providing transactions for Bank Mellat and EIH in support of Iran's proliferation activities.

China, Russia, and Others

The position of Russia, China, and several other countries—that they will impose only those sanctions required by applicable U.N. Security Council resolutions, but not impose sanctions beyond those specifically mandated—has been of concern to several Members of Congress. Asnoted below, some Members and outside experts express concern that Chinese firms, in particular, might move to fill the void in Iran's energy industry left by vacating European firms ("backfill"), but administration officials say they have not seen evidence of such a trend. Russia is an oil exporter itself and a need to preserve oil imports from Iran are therefore not a factor in its Iran policy calculations.

At the same time, there are no signs that China would join an EU-led embargo of purchases of Iranian oil. About 20% of Iran's total oil exports are to China – with a value of about $16 billion in 2011. That is more than sufficient to offset the approximately $12 billion in goods Iran buys from China, meaning that China has to settle some of this trade balance in hard currency. Treasury Department officials say China does not make extensive use of payments through Iran's Central Bank, but alternative mechanisms that are used are unclear. Some speculate that China might be making some payments to Iran in its own currency or other currencies.

An even more significant concern is that these and other countries are refusing or failing to prevent Iran from acquiring weapons and WMD technology. Secretary of State Clinton singled out China on January 19, 2011, as not enforcing all aspects of international sanctions that bar sales of most nuclear-related equipment to Iran; the comment came of the eve of the state visit to the United States by President Hu Jintao. On March 9, 2011, State Department Special Adviser for Non-Proliferation and Arms Control, Robert Einhorn, said Iran may be working with Chinese firms to obtain sensitive technology useful for nuclear weapons development. In some cases, Iran has been able, according to some reports, to obtain sophisticated technology even from U.S. firms.[42]

A related issue is Iran's efforts to use the high seas or the territory of other countries to supply weapons to groups it supports (such shipments are barred by U.N. resolutions; see above). In March 2011, Israel intercepted a freighter, the *Victoria*, that it said was carrying Iranian weapons to Palestinian militant groups. Also in March 2011, Turkey, generally considered friendly toward Iran, complied with U.N. requirements by twice forcing the landing in Turkey of Iranian cargo aircraft. In both cases, the aircraft were searched, and in one instance, weapons were removed, allegedly bound for Syria, before the aircraft were allowed to proceed.

Contrast with Previous Periods

The emerging consensus on Iran sanctions differs from early periods when there was far more disagreement. Reflecting the traditional European preference for providing incentives rather than enacting economic punishments, during 2002-2005, there were active negotiations between the European Union and Iran on a "Trade and Cooperation Agreement" (TCA). Such an agreement would have lowered the tariffs or increased quotas for Iranian exports to the EU countries.[43]

However, negotiations were discontinued after the election of Ahmadinejad in June 2005, at which time Iran's position on its nuclear program hardened. Similarly, there is insufficient international support to grant Iran membership in the World Trade Organization (WTO) until there is progress on the nuclear issue. Iran first attempted to apply to join the WTO in July 1996. On 22 occasions after that, representatives of the Clinton and then the George W. Bush administration blocked Iran from applying (applications must be by consensus of the 148 members). As discussed above, as part of an effort to assist the EU-3 nuclear talks with Iran, at a WTO meeting in May 2005, no opposition to Iran's application was registered, and Iran formally began accession talks.

Earlier, during the 1990s, EU countries maintained a policy of "critical dialogue" with Iran, and the EU and Japan refused to join the 1995 U.S. trade and investment ban on Iran.

The European dialogue with Iran was suspended in April 1997 in response to the German terrorism trial ("Mykonos trial") that found high-level Iranian involvement in killing Iranian dissidents in Germany, but resumed in May 1998 during Khatemi's presidency.

In the 1990s, European and Japanese creditors—over U.S. objections—rescheduled about $16 billion in Iranian debt. These countries (governments and private creditors) rescheduled the debt bilaterally, in spite of Paris Club rules that call for multilateral rescheduling.

In July 2002, Iran tapped international capital markets for the first time since the Islamic revolution, selling $500 million in bonds to European banks. (A provision of H.R. 6296 would make sanctionable under ISA the purchase of Iranian sovereign debt).

World Bank Loans

The July 27, 2010, EU measures narrowed substantially the prior differences between the EU and the United States over international lending to Iran. As noted above, the United States representative to international financial institutions is required to vote against international lending, but that vote, although weighted, is not sufficient to block international lending. In 1993 the United States voted its 16.5% share of the World Bank against loans to Iran of $460 million for electricity, health, and irrigation projects, but the loans were approved. To block that lending, the FY1994-FY1996 foreign aid appropriations (P.L. 103-87, P.L. 103-306, and P.L. 104-107) cut the amount appropriated for the U.S. contribution to the bank by the amount of those loans. The legislation contributed to a temporary halt in new bank lending to Iran. (In the 111th Congress, a provision of H.R. 6296—Title VII—cut off U.S. contributions to the World Bank, International Finance Corp., and the Multilateral Investment Guarantee Corp. if the World Bank approves a new Country Assistance Strategy for Iran or makes a loan to Iran.)

During 1999-2005, Iran's moderating image had led the World Bank to consider new loans over U.S. opposition. In May 2000, the United States' allies outvoted the United States to approve $232 million in loans for health and sewage projects. During April 2003-May 2005, a total of $725 million in loans were approved for environmental management, housing reform, water and sanitation projects, and land management projects, in addition to $400 million in loans for earthquake relief.

Table 4. Points of Comparison between U.S., U.N., and EU Sanctions against Iran

U.S. Sanctions	U.N. Sanctions	Implementation by EU (July 27, 2010) and Some Allied Countries
General Observation: Most sweeping sanctions on Iran of virtually any country in the world	General Observation: Most sweeping sanctions on Iran of virtually any country in the world	EU abides by all U.N. sanctions on Iran, but new package of Iran sanctions announced July 27, 2010, more closely aligns EU sanctions with those of the U.S. than ever before. Japan and South Korean sanctions (September 2010) similar to EU.
Ban on U.S. Trade with and Investment in Iran:	U.N. sanctions do not ban civilian trade with Iran or general civilian sector.	No general EU ban on trade in civilian goods with Iran, although the July 27, 2010,
Executive Order 12959 bans (with limited exceptions) U.S. firms from exporting to Iran, importing from Iran, or investing in Iran. There is an exemption for sales to Iran of food and medical products, but no trade financing or financing guarantees are permitted.	investment in Iran. Nor do U.N. sanctions mandate restrictions on provision of trade financing or financing guarantees by national export credit guarantee agencies	sanctions ban sales of energy related equipment and services. On May 23, 2011, the EU named about 100 entities as Iran proliferation-related entities which EU entities would be unable to do business with. EU, Japan, and South Korea measures ban "medium and long term" trade financing and financing guarantees. Short term financing is permitted, but there is a call for EU states to "exercise restraint" on that.
Do Business With Iran's Energy Sector: The Iran Sanctions Act, P.L. 104-172 (as amended most recently by the Comprehensive Iran Sanctions, Accountability, and Divestment Act of 2010, P.L. 111-195), and as enhanced by Executive Order 13590, mandates specified sanctions on foreign firms that invest threshold amounts in Iran's	No U.N. equivalent exists. However, preambular language in Resolution 1929 "not[es] the potential connection between Iran's revenues derived from its energy sector and the funding of Iran's proliferation-sensitive nuclear activities." This wording is interpreted by most observers as providing U.N. support for countries	July 27, 2010, EU sanctions prohibit EU companies from financing energy sector projects in Iran (a de-facto ban on energy sector investment) and ban sales to Iran of equipment or services for its energy sector, including projects outside Iran. No ban on buying oil or gas from Iran or selling gasoline to Iran, but such a step is under consideration as of late 2011.

U.S. Sanctions	U.N. Sanctions	Implementation by EU (July 27, 2010) and Some Allied Countries
energy Sector or that sell certain threshold amounts of refined petroleum, or equipment or services for oil and gas development, refinery or petrochemical plant expansion or maintenance, or production or importation of gasoline.	who want to ban their companies from investing in Iran's energy sector.	Japan and South Korean measures ban new energy projects in Iran and call for restraint on ongoing projects.
Ban on Foreign Assistance: U.S. foreign assistance to Iran—other than purely humanitarian aid— is banned under Section 620A of the Foreign Assistance Act . That section bans U.S. assistance to countries on the U.S. list of "state sponsors of terrorism." Iran has been on this "terrorism list" since January 1984. Iran is also routinely denied direct U.S. foreign aid under the annual foreign operations appropriations acts (most recently in Section 7007 of division H of P.L. 111-8).	No U.N. equivalent	EU measures of July 27, 2010, ban grants, aid, and concessional loans to Iran. Also prohibit financing of enterprises involved in Iran's energy sector. Japan and South Korea measures did not specifically ban aid or lending to Iran.
Ban on Arms Exports to Iran: Because Iran is on the "terrorism list," it is ineligible for U.S. arms exports pursuant to Section 40 of the Arms Export Control Act (AECA, P.L. 95-92). The International Trafficking in Arms Regulations (ITAR, 22 CFR Part 126.1) also cite the president's authority to control arms exports, and to comply with U.N. Security Council Resolutions as a justification to ban arms exports and imports.	Resolution 1929 (operative paragraph 8) bans all U.N. member states from selling or supplying to Iran major weapons systems, including tanks, armored vehicles, combat aircraft, warships, and most missile systems, or related spare parts or advisory services for such weapons systems.	EU sanctions include a comprehensive ban on sale to Iran of all types of military equipment, not just major combat systems. No similar Japan and South Korean measures announced, but neither has exported arms to Iran.
Restriction on Exports to Iran of "Dual Use Items": Primarily under Section 6(j) of the Export Administration Act (P.L. 96- 72) and Section 38 of the Arms Export Control Act, there is a denial of license applications to sell Iran goods that could have military applications.	The U.N. Resolutions on Iran, cumulatively, ban the export of almost all dual-use items to Iran.	EU bans the sales of dual use items to Iran, in line with U.N. resolutions. Japan announced full adherence to strict export control regimes when evaluating sales to Iran.

Table 4. (Continued)

U.S. Sanctions	U.N. Sanctions	Implementation by EU (July 27, 2010) and Some Allied Countries
Sanctions Against International Lending to Iran: Under Section 1621 of the International Financial Institutions Act (P.L. 95-118), U.S. representatives to international financial institutions, such as the World Bank, are required to vote against loans to Iran by those institutions.	Resolution 1747 (oper. paragraph 7) requests, but does not mandate, that countries and international financial institutions refrain from making grants or loans to Iran, except for development and humanitarian purposes.	The July 27, 2010, measures prohibit EU members from providing grants, aid, and concessional loans to Iran, including through international financial institutions. No specific similar Japan or South Korea measures announced.
Sanctions Against Foreign Firms that Sell Weapons of Mass Destruction-Related Technology to Iran: Several laws and regulations, including the Iran-Syria North Korea Nonproliferation Act (P.L. 106-178), the Iran-Iraq Arms Nonproliferation Act (P.L. 102-484) and Executive Order 13382 provide for sanctions against entities, Iranian or otherwise, that are determined to be involved in or supplying Iran's WMD programs (asset freezing, ban on transaction with the entity).	Resolution 1737 (oper. paragraph 12) imposes a worldwide freeze on the assets and property of Iranian entities named in an Annex to the Resolution. Each subsequent Resolution has expanded the list of Iranian entities subject to these sanctions.	The EU measures imposed July 27, 2010, commit the EU to freezing the assets of entities named in the U.N. resolutions, as well as numerous other named Iranian entities. Japan and South Korea froze assets of U.N.-sanctioned entities.
Ban on Transactions With Terrorism Supporting Entities: Executive Order 13224 bans transactions with entities determined by the Administration to be supporting international terrorism. Numerous entities, including some of Iranian origin, have been so designated.	No direct equivalent The U.N. Resolutions against Iran are intended primarily to slow or halt Iran's nuclear and other WMD programs. However, Resolution 1747 (oper. paragraph 5) bans Iran from exporting any arms—a provision widely interpreted as trying to reduce Iran's material support to groups such as Lebanese Hizbollah, Hamas, Shiite militias in Iraq, and insurgents in Afghanistan.	No direct equivalent, but EU measures taken July 27, 2010, include some IRGC Qods Force and related persons and entities as subject to a freeze on EU-based assets. Another 180 such entities designated by the EU on December 1, 2011.
Travel Ban on Named Iranians: The Comprehensive Iran Sanctions, Accountability, and Divestment Act of 2010 (P.L. 111-195) provides for a	Resolution 1803 imposed a binding ban on international travel by several Iranians named in an Annex to the Resolution. Resolution 1929 extended that	The EU sanctions announced July 27, 2010, contains an Annex of named Iranians subject to a ban on travel to the EU countries. An additional 32

U.S. Sanctions	U.N. Sanctions	Implementation by EU (July 27, 2010) and Some Allied Countries
prohibition on travel to the U.S. , blocking of U.S.-based property, and ban on transactions with Iranians determined to be involved in serious human rights abuses against Iranians since the June 12, 2009, presidential election there.	ban to additional Iranians, and forty Iranians are now subject to the ban. However, the Iranians subject to the travel ban are so subjected because of their involvement in Iran's WMD programs, not because of involvement in human rights abuses.	Iranians involved in human rights abuses were subjected to EU sanctions on April 14, 2011. Japan and South Korea announced bans on named Iranians.
Restrictions on Iranian Shipping: Under Executive Order 13382, the U.S. Treasury Department has named Islamic Republic of Iran Shipping Lines and several affiliated entities as entities whose U.S.-based property is to be frozen.	Resolution 1803 and 1929 authorize countries to inspect cargoes carried by Iran Air and Islamic Republic of Iran Shipping Lines (IRISL)—or any ships in national or international waters—if there is an indication that the shipments include goods whose export to Iran is banned.	The EU measures announced July 27, 2010, bans Iran Air Cargo from access to EU airports. The measures also freeze the EU-based assets of IRISL and its affiliates. Insurance and re-insurance for Iranian firms is banned. Japan and South Korean measures take similar actions against IRISL and Iran Air.
Banking Sanctions: A number or provisions and policies have been employed to persuade foreign banks to end their relationships with Iranian banks. Several Iranian banks have been named as proliferation or terrorism supporting entities under Executive Orders 13382 and 13224, respectively.	No direct equivalent However, two Iranian banks are named as sanctioned entities under the U.N. Security Council resolutions.	The EU announcement on July 27, 2010, prohibit the opening in EU countries of any new branches or offices of Iranian banks. The measures also prohibit EU banks from offices or accounts in Iran. In addition, the transfer of funds exceeding 40,000 Euros (about $50,000) between and Iranian bank and an EU bank require prior authorization by EU bank regulators. Japan and South Korea measures similar to the above, with South Korea adhering to the same 40,000 Euro authorization requirement. Japan and S. Korea froze the assets of 15 Iranian banks; South Korea targeted Bank Mellat for freeze.
No direct equivalent, although, as discussed above, U.S. proliferations laws provide for sanctions against foreign entities that help Iran with its nuclear and ballistic missile programs.	Resolution 1929 (oper. paragraph 7) prohibits Iran from acquiring an interest in any country involving uranium mining, production, or use of nuclear materials, or technology related to nuclear-capable ballistic missiles.	EU measures on July 27, 2010, require adherence to this provision of Resolution 1929.

Table 4. (Continued)

U.S. Sanctions	U.N. Sanctions	Implementation by EU (July 27, 2010) and Some Allied Countries
	Operative Paragraph 9 of Resolution 1929 prohibits Iran from undertaking "any activity" related to ballistic missiles capable of delivering a nuclear weapon.	

EFFECTS OF SANCTIONS ON IRAN

Assessing the effectiveness of U.S. and international sanctions on depends at least in part upon which goals are being examined. U.S. officials acknowledge that the sanctions have not achieved the core goal of altering Iran's commitment to its nuclear program. However, most outside experts agree that the sanctions are contributing to the necessary, if not sufficient, subordinate goal of applying increasing pressure to Iran's economy. Iran's political system is in turmoil, and there is domestic pressure on the regime to reform or change outright, but this sentiment appears to be caused by factors not directly related to Iran's economy or to international sanctions.

At various conferences, some administration officials have urged to allow time for the existing sanctions to work but, following the October 2011 revelation of the alleged Iranian plot against the Saudi Ambassador to the United States and the November 8, 2011, IAEA report focused on possibly nuclear weapons design efforts, administration officials are pushing for additional multi-national sanctions – an outcome of which was the November 21, 2011, coordinated U.S., British, and Canadian announcement of new sanctions against Iran's financial sector. At the same time, the administration maintains that sanctions be properly targeted and calibrated so as not to cause a sudden spike in world oil prices.

Effect on Nuclear Negotiations

There is a consensus that U.S. and U.N. sanctions have not, to date, accomplished their core strategic objective of causing a demonstrable shift in Iran's commitment to its nuclear program. Most experts assess that the optimal means for sanctions to affect the nuclear program is by compelling an Iran decision to accept a compromise that would limit Iran's nuclear development. In late November 2010, Iran accepted new nuclear talks in Geneva. However, during two days of talks (December 6 and 7, 2010), Iran did not agree to curbs on its enrichment of uranium, the core U.S. demand. There was an agreement to have new talks in Turkey, which took place during January 21-22, 2011. Those talks, by all accounts, made little progress as Iran refused to discuss details of various proposals for nuclear confidence building measures. The talks were said to have nearly broken down at the end of the first day. An exchange of letters between Iran and the EU foreign policy representative (acting on behalf of the P5+1) during February-May 2011 did not indicate sufficient Iranian flexibility to prompt the P5+1 to seek to schedule new talks with Iran.

Some might argue that the assessment of the effect of sanctions on Iran's negotiating stance might be subject to reassessment. In August 2011, Iranian officials indicated interest in Russian proposals to restart talks and indicated a willingness to allow closer IAEA "supervision" or inspections of Iran's nuclear program. President Ahmadinejad, during his September 2011 U.N. General Assembly visit to the United States, said Iran might accept a proposal to cap the level of its uranium enrichment at 5%. These statements could represent new flexibility and indicate that sanctions might be causing Iranian leaders to seek to reduce international pressure. However, as of early December 2011, no new P5+1 talks with Iran are scheduled, and none are likely in light of the virtual break in Iran-Britain relations sparked by the Iranian storming of Britain's Embassy in Tehran.

Counter-Proliferation Effects

A related issue is whether the cumulative sanctions have, in and of themselves, added bottlenecks to Iran's nuclear efforts by making it difficult for Iran to import needed materials or skills. In a speech on November 22, 2011, National Security Adviser Tom Donilon said:

> The effect of these sanctions has been clear. Coupled with mistakes and difficulties in Iran, they have slowed Iran's nuclear efforts. Sanctions and export control efforts have made it more difficult and costly for Iran to acquire key materials and equipment for its enrichment program, including items that Iran cannot produce itself.[44]

Others, however, say that there is not clear evidence that sanctions are slowing Iran's program in that International Atomic Energy Agency (IAEA) reports say that Iran's stockpile of low-enriched uranium continues to expand,[45] as do its holdings of 20% enriched uranium. This latter material is a cause of U.S. concern because of the technological skill needed to produce that level of enrichment.

General Political Effects

The international community has hoped that international sanctions might widen splits in Iran's leadership and cause its leaders to reconsider major foreign policy decisions, particularly the nuclear program. There are growing indications of splits in the Iranian leadership—particularly between President Ahmadinejad and the Supreme Leader—to the point at which there has been open discussion in Iran's parliament since June 2011 of impeaching Ahmadinejad. In October 2011, the Supreme Leader raised the possibility of amending Iran's constitution to eliminate the post of president altogether, and replace it with a parliamentary system in which the *Majles* selects a Prime Minister. However, this split does not appear to be driven primarily by differences over economic policy or how to react to international sanctions.

At the broader level, in early 2011, the opposition Green movement returned to the streets in a few significant protests. However, the protests were not been sustained since and there is no evidence that international sanctions are affecting the strength of the domestic opposition either positively or negatively. The opposition is driven by long-standing political grievances and has not, to date, been joined by labor groups or other protesters articulating purely economic or foreign policy demands. Some argue that difficult economic conditions are contributing to the political quiescence of Iranian labor because the working class fears loss of pay from participation in demonstrations or from regime retaliation.

There have been anecdotal reports of unrest in 2011, including strikes by laborers for overdue pay and shuttering of stores by merchants who are having trouble obtaining trade financing, insurance, and shipping availability. These difficulties are driving up their costs by an estimated 40%, even if the merchants can complete desired transactions at all.[46] A substantial portion of the Iranian economy depends on import-export activity, so the damage to the merchant community from international sanctions has been considerable. Labor strikes were also key to the 1979 downfall of the Shah's rule, and are closely watched by the regime for signs of spreading or drawing in other groups to their cause.

Economic Effects

An IMF study issued in August 2011 casts some doubt that international sanctions are seriously harming Iran's economy.[47] The study, based largely on a May 28-June 9, 2011 study visit, indicated that Iran's GDP is growing at a rate of about 3.5% and is expected to increase to about 4.5% in the medium term. The study also credits positive economic effects to the government's privatization program. The report also concurs with the view of many experts that high world oil prices remain—above $100 per barrel in early December 2011—enable the regime to mitigate the effects of international sanctions.

Despite the high oil prices, U.S. officials, including National Security Adviser Donilon in the speech cited above, believe that sanctions are causing Iran's economy to perform well below its potential (high unemployment, for example) and vulnerable to downturn as U.S. and partner strategy shuts Iran out of the global financial system, raises the costs for Iran of financing its transactions, causes international firms to exit Iran, and threatens to reduce Iran's oil sales.

And, Iranian officials have said that sanctions are hurting Iran's economy: President Ahmadinejad told Iran's *Majles* (parliament) on November 1, 2011, that international sanctions are causing serious problems for Iran's banking sector.

Iran's Finance Minister made similar comments at the end of November. Among other specifics:

- During 2006 and 2010, Treasury and State Departments officials say they persuaded at least 80 banks not to process transactions for Iranian banks. Among those that have pulled out of Iran are UBS (Switzerland), HSBC (Britain), Germany's Commerzbank A.G., and Deutsche Bank AG. U.S. financial diplomacy has reportedly convinced Kuwaiti banks to stop transactions with Iranian accounts,[48] and some banks in Asia (primarily South Korea and Japan) and the rest of the Middle East have done the same. Then-Under Secretary Levey said on September 20, 2010, that "today, Iran is effectively unable to access financial services from reputable banks and is increasingly unable to conduct major transactions in dollars or Euros."[49]

- As noted above, the banking sanctions have created difficulty for several of Iran's oil customers to process payments to Iran. These payments difficulties have left Iran's Central Bank short of hard currency and caused a reduction in the value of the currency, by many accounts. Earlier, in September 2010, the value of Iran's currency, the rial, fell by about 15% when the UAE, a major financial hub for Iran, began restricting transactions with Iranian banks sanctioned by U.N. resolutions and by the United States.
- Treasury Department's designations of affiliates and ships belong to Islamic Republic of Iran Shipping Lines (IRISL) reportedly are harming Iran's ability to ship goods and raised the prices of goods to Iranian import-export dealers. Some ships have been impounded by various countries for nonpayment of debts due on them.

Foreign Companies Exiting the Iran Market

Because the international community has sought to isolate Iran economically, companies all over the world have come to a decision to end their business with Iran, even when such business would not appear to violate any U.N. or national sanction. Neither the U.S. ban on trade and investment with Iran, nor U.N. sanctions, nor European Union sanctions on Iran, ban trade with Iran in all civilian goods. Many experts believe that, over time, the efficiency and output of Iran's economy will decline as foreign expertise departs and Iran attracts alternative investment from or imports goods from less capable foreign companies. Examples of major non-U.S. companies discontinuing business with Iran include the following:

- ABB of Switzerland said in January 2010 it would cease doing business with Iran.
- Siemens of Germany was active in the Iran telecommunications infrastructure market, but announced in February 2010 that it would cease pursuing business in Iran. Finemeccanica, a defense and transportation conglomerate of Italy, followed suit, as did Thyssen-Krupp, a German steelmaker.
- Germany's Daimler (Mercedes-Benz maker) said in April 2010 it would freeze planned exports to Iran of cars and trucks.

- In August-September 2010, Japan and South Korea announced that their automakers Toyota, Hyundai, and Kia Motors would cease selling automobiles to Iran.
- Attorneys for BNP Paribas of France told the author in July 2011 that, as of 2007, the firm was pursuing no new business in Iran, although it was fulfilling existing obligations in that market.
- On June 30, 2011, according to press reports, the Danish shipping giant Maersk told Iran that it would no longer operate out of Iran's three largest ports. The firm's decision reportedly was based on the U.S. announcement on June 23, 2011, that it was sanctioning the operator of those ports, Tidewater Middle East Co., as a proliferation entity under Executive Order 13382. The pullout of Maersk will likely further raise shipping costs.

Foreign Firms Reportedly Remaining in the Iran Market

Some firms continue to run the financial risk of doing business with Iran. Some of the well-known firms that continue to do so include Alcatel-Lucent of France; Bank of Tokyo-Mitsubishi UFJ; Bosch of Germany; Canon of Japan; Fiat SPA of Italy; Ericsson of Sweden; ING Group of the Netherlands; Mercedes of Germany; Renault of France; Samsung of South Korea; Sony of Japan; Volkswagen of Germany; Volvo of Sweden; and numerous others. Some of the foreign firms that trade with Iran, such as Mitsui and Co. of Japan, Alstom of France, and Schneider Electric of France, are discussed in the March 7, 2010, *New York Times* article on foreign firms that do business with Iran and also receive U.S. contracts or financing. The *Times* article does not claim that these firms have violated any U.S. sanctions laws.

Other questions have arisen over how U.S. sanctions might apply to business with foreign firms that Iran might acquire a full or partial interest in. Such firms include Daewoo Electronics of South Korea, where an Iranian firm—Entekhab Industrial Corp.—is a leading bidder to take over that firm. Another example is Adabank of Turkey, which reportedly might be sold to Iran.

Subsidy Phase-Out Issue

A larger issue, which may have been affected by sanctions, but perhaps positively for Iran, is a long-delayed plan to phase out state subsidies on staple goods such staples as gasoline and some foods over the next five years. International sanctions might have helped Ahmadinejad convince the Majles (parliament) that passing the subsidy reduction plan was urgent if Iran was to parry the effects of burgeoning international sanctions. After several delays, the program started on December 19, 2010, with a reduction in subsidies of gasoline and bread. The price of traditional bread immediately escalated to 40 cents, from 15 cents, when the program began. Gasoline prices now run on a tiered system in which a small increment is available at the subsidized price of about 1.60 per gallon, but amounts above that threshold are available only at a price of about $2.60 per gallon, close to the world price. The lower and lower middle class is being compensated with direct cash payments of about $40 per month.[50]

The IMF report of August 2011, discussed above, said that the phase-out removed about $60 billion in costs from Iran's budget. The report also credits the regime with successfully containing initial impact of the rise in domestic energy prices on inflation. However, some Iranian economists say that 63 million Iranians qualify for the compensatory cash payments and that this costs the government nearly all of the savings incurred from the subsidy phase-out.

Nor has the subsidy phase out produced major additional unrest. When the plan went into effect in December 2010, some Iranian truckers simply stopped working on the grounds that their work was no longer profitable (because the government limited the amount of extra fees that can be charged to make up for the increase in costs). However, the subsidy phase out did not produce new Green movement demonstrations or other indicators of opposition.

Effect on the Energy Sector

As noted throughout, the U.S. objective has been to target sanctions against Iran's energy sector, considered the engine of Iran's economy. The sector is the source of nearly 70% of government revenue. Depriving the regime of substantial revenue, it is believed, will reduce its ability to import needed technology for its WMD programs and enlist and maintain the loyalty of security personnel.

There are clear indications that the sanctions—coupled with the overall sense that Iran is isolated from the international community—are causing substantial injury to the energy sector.

U.S. officials in 2011 say that Iran has lost close to $60 billion in investment as numerous major firms have either announced pullouts from some of their Iran projects, declined to make further investments, or resold their investments to other companies. On the other hand, Treasury official

David Cohen, mentioned above, testified in October 2011 that sanctions are likely to deprive Iran of an estimated $14 billion in oil revenue from 2011 to 2016.

Observers at key energy fields in Iran say there is little evidence of foreign investment activity and little new development activity sighted, including at the large South Pars gas field that Iran has focused on for at least 10 years. It is highly unlikely that Iran will attract the $145 billion in new investment by 2018 that Iran's deputy Oil Minister said in November 2008 that Iran needs. Similar estimates come from independent Iranian energy experts, who say that, as of October 2011, the sector needs $130 billion in investment from 2011 until 2020.[51] A Government Accountability Office (GAO) report of August 3, 2011, contains tables that discuss those firms that have discontinued commercial activity in Iran's energy sector, as well as those still operating and investing.[52] *Table 3* shows international firms that have invested or remain invested in Iran's energy sector. Some of them have not been determined to have violated ISA and may be under investigation by the State Department. As discussed above, some firms have been sanctioned, and others have avoided sanctions either through administration waivers or invocation of the "special rule."

Possibly or partly as a result of the relative lack of new investment, Iran's oil production has remain relatively steady at about 4.1 million barrels per day (mbd) since the mid-2000s, despite government efforts to expand production. Production is projected to fall to about 3.3 mbd by 2015.[53] That estimate is somewhat less than the 25% decline over the next five years (by 2016) that the GAO August 3, 2011, report, quoting Oil and Gas Journal, estimates is possible. Others maintain that Iran's gas sector can compensate for declining oil exports, although Iran has used its gas development primarily to reinject into its oil fields rather than to export. Iran exports about 3.6 trillion cubic feet of gas, primarily to Turkey, but also to Armenia. Some Members of Congress believe that ISA would have been even more effective in injuring Iran's energy sector if successive administrations had imposed ISA sanctions more aggressively.

The EU sanctions apparently have also derailed a BP-NIOC joint venture in the Rhum gas field, 200 miles off the coast of Scotland. BP announced in November 2010 that it would stop production there to ensure compliance with the EU sanctions. In addition, partners in the Trans-Adriatic Pipeline (TAP) said in September 2010 that the pipeline would not be used to transport Iranian gas to Europe.

Some believed that a key to further harming Iran's energy sector is to persuade remaining oil services firms to pull out of Iran. In press articles and in the December 1, 2010, House Foreign Affairs Committee hearing discussed above, the large oil services firm Schlumberger, which in incorporated in the Netherlands Antilles, has said it will wind down its business with Iran. However, press reports citing company documents say all contracts with Iran might not be terminated until at least 2013.[54] Persuading other oil services firms to exit Iran was the intent of Executive Order 13590 of November 21, 2011, which makes such activity sanctionable.

Concerns about "Backfill"

There has been a concern that some of the investment void might be "backfilled," at least partly, by Asian firms such as those from China, Malaysia, Vietnam, and countries in Eastern Europe. However, many such deals are said to be in preliminary stages, and clear examples of "backfilling" are few, to date. Most of the companies that might backfill abandoned projects are perceived as not being as technically capable as those that have withdrawn from Iran. In July 2010, after the enactment of Resolution 1929 and CISADA, the Revolutionary Guard's main construction affiliate, Khatem ol-Anbiya, announced it had withdrawn from developing Phases 15 and 16 of South Pars—a project worth $2 billion.[55] Khatem ol-Anbiya took over that project in 2006 when Norway's Kvaerner pulled out of it. It is likely that the IRGC perceived its involvement as likely to scare away foreign participation in the work because U.S. and U.N. sanctions are targeting the IRGC and its corporate affiliates.

Table 5. Post-1999 Major Investments/Major Development Projects in Iran's Energy Sector

Date	Field/Project	Company(ies)/Status (If Known)	Value	Output/Goal
February 1999	Doroud (oil) (Energy Information Agency, Department of Energy, August 2006.) Total and ENI exempted from sanctions on September 30 because of pledge to exit Iran market	Total (France)/ENI (Italy)	$1 billion	205,000 bpd
April 1999	Balal (oil) ("Balal Field Development in Iran Completed," *World Market Research Centre*, May 17, 2004.)	Total/ Bow Valley (Canada)/ENI	$300 million	40,000 bpd

Date	Field/Project	Company(ies)/Status (If Known)	Value	Output/Goal
Nov. 1999	Soroush and Nowruz (oil) ("News in Brief: Iran." *Middle East Economic Digest*, (MEED) January 24, 2003.) Royal Dutch exempted from sanctions on 9/30 because of pledge to exit Iran market	Royal Dutch Shell (Netherlands)/Japex (Japan)	\$800 million	190,000 bpd
April 2000	Anaran bloc (oil) (MEED Special Report, December 16, 2005, pp. 48-50.)	Norsk Hydro and Statoil (Norway) and Gazprom and Lukoil (Russia) No production to date; Statoil and Norsk have left project.	\$105 million	65,000
July 2000	Phase 4 and 5, South Pars (gas) (*Petroleum Economist*, December 1, 2004.) ENI exempted 9/30 based on pledge to exit Iran market	ENI Gas onstream as of Dec. 2004	\$1.9 billion	2 billion cu.ft./day (cfd)
March 2001	Caspian Sea oil exploration—construction of submersible drilling rig for Iranian partner (IPR Strategic Business Information Database, March 11, 2001.)	GVA Consultants (Sweden)	\$225 million	NA
June 2001	Darkhovin (oil) ("Darkhovin Production Doubles." Gulf Daily News, May 1, 2008.) ENI told CRS in April 2010 it would close out all Iran operations by 2013. ENI exempted from sanctions on 9/30, as discussed above	ENI Field in production	\$1 billion	100,000 bpd
May 2002	Masjid-e-Soleyman (oil) ("CNPC Gains Upstream Foothold." MEED, September 3, 2004.)	Sheer Energy (Canada)/China National Petroleum Company (CNPC). Local partner is Naftgaran Engineering	\$80 million	25,000 bpd
Sept. 2002	Phase 9 + 10, South Pars (gas) ("OIEC Surpasses South Korean Company in South Pars." IPR Strategic Business Information Database, November 15, 2004.)	LG Engineering and Construction Corp. (now known as GS Engineering and Construction Corp., South Korea) On stream as of early 2009	\$1.6 billion	2 billion cfd

Table 5. (Continued)

Date	Field/Project	Company(ies)/Status (If Known)	Value	Output/Goal
October 2002	Phase 6, 7, 8, South Pars (gas) (Source: Statoil, May 2011) Field began producing late 2008; operational control handed to NIOC in 2009. Statoil exempted from sanctions on 9/30/2010 because Statoil pledged to exit Iran market.	Statoil (Norway)	$750 million	3 billion cfd
January 2004	Azadegan (oil) ("Japan Mulls Azadegan Options." APS Review Oil Market Trends, November 27, 2006.) October 15, 2010: Inpex announced it would exit the project by selling its stake; "special rule" exempting it from ISA investigation invoked November 17, 2010.	Inpex (Japan) 10% stake. CNPC agreed to develop "north Azadegan" in Jan. 2009	$200 million (Inpex stake); China $1.76 billion	260,000 bpd
August 2004	Tusan Block Oil found in block in Feb. 2009, but not in commercial quantity, according to the firm. ("Iran-Petrobras Operations." APS Review Gas Market Trends, April 6, 2009; "Brazil's Petrobras Sees Few Prospects for Iran Oil,"(http://www.reuters.com/article/idUSN0317110720090703.)	Petrobras (Brazil)	$178 million	No production
October 2004	Yadavaran (oil) Formal start of development of the field still delayed as of September 2011 ("China Curbs Iran Energy Work, Reuters, September 2, 2011)	Sinopec (China), deal finalized December 9, 2007	$2 billion	300,000 bpd
2005	Saveh bloc (oil) GAO report, cited below	PTT (Thailand)	?	?
June 2006	Garmsar bloc (oil) Deal finalized in June 2009 ("China's Sinopec signs a deal to develop oil block in Iran—report," Forbes, 20 June 2009, http://www.forbes.com/feeds/afx/2006/06/20/afx2829188.html.)	Sinopec (China)	$20 million	?

Date	Field/Project	Company(ies)/Status (If Known)	Value	Output/Goal
July 2006	Arak Refinery expansion (GAO reports; Fimco FZE Machinery website; http://www.fimco.org/ index.php? option=com_content&task=view&id =70& Itemid=78.)	Sinopec (China); JGC (Japan). Work may have been taken over or continued by Hyundai Heavy Industries (S. Korea)	$959 million (major initial expansion; extent of Hyundai work unknown)	Expansion to produce 250,000 bpd
Sept. 2006	Khorramabad block (oil) Seismic data gathered, but no production is planned. (Statoil factsheet, May 2011)	Norsk Hydro and Statoil (Norway).	$49 million	?
Feb. 2007	LNG Tanks at Tombak Port Contract to build three LNG tanks at Tombak, 30 miles north of Assaluyeh Port. (May not constitute "investment" as defined in pre-2010 version of ISA, because that definition did not specify LNG as "petroleum resource" of Iran.) "Central Bank Approves $900 Million for Iran LNG Project." Tehran Times, June 13, 2009.	Daelim (S. Korea)	$320 million	200,000 ton capacity
March 2007	Esfahan refinery upgrade ("Daelim, Others to Upgrade Iran's Esfahan Refinery." *Chemical News and Intelligence,* March 19, 2007.)	Daelim (S. Korea)		NA
Dec. 2007	Golshan and Ferdows onshore and offshore gas fields and LNG plant contract modified but reaffirmed December 2008 (GAO report; Oil Daily, January 14, 2008.)	SKS Ventures, Petrofield Subsidiary (Malaysia)	$16 billion	3.4 billion cfd
2007 (unspec.)	Jofeir Field (oil) GAO report cited below. Belarusneft, a subsidiary of Belneftekhim, sanctioned under ISA on March 29, 2011. Naftiran sanctioned on September 29, 2010, for this and other activities.	Belarusneft (Belarus) under contract to Naftiran. No production to date	$500 million	40,000 bpd
2008	Dayyer Bloc (Persian Gulf, offshore, oil) GAO report cited below	Edison (Italy)	$44 million	?

Table 5. (Continued)

Date	Field/Project	Company(ies)/Status (If Known)	Value	Output/Goal
February 2008	Lavan field (offshore natural gas) GAO report cited below	PGNiG (Poland) Status unclear	$2 billion	
March 2008	Danan Field (on-shore oil) "PVEP Wins Bid to Develop Danan Field." Iran Press TV, March 11, 2008	Petro Vietnam Exploration and Production Co. (Vietnam)	?	?
April 2008	Moghan 2 (onshore oil and gas, Ardebil province) GAO report cited below	INA (Croatia)	$40-$140 million (dispute over size)	?
?	Kermanshah petrochemical plant (new construction) GAO report cited below	Uhde (Germany)		300,000 metric tons/yr
January 2009	"North Azadegan" (Chinadaily.com. "CNPC to Develop Azadegan Oilfield," http://www.chinadaily.com.cn/bizchina/2009-1/16/content_ 7403699.htm.)	CNPC (China)	$1.75 billion	75,000 bpd
January 2009	Bushehr Polymer Plants Production of polyethelene at two polymer plants in Bushehr Province (GAO August 2011 report)	Sasol (South Africa)	?	Capacity is 1 million tons per year. Products are exported from Iran.
Nov. 2009	South Pars: Phase 12—Part 2 and Part 3 ("Italy, South Korea To Develop South Pars Phase 12." Press TV (Iran), November 3, 2009, http://www.presstv. com/pop/Print/?id=110308.)	Daelim (S. Korea)—Part 2; Tecnimont (Italy)—Part 3	$4 billion ($2 bn each part)	
February 2010	South Pars: Phase 11 Drilling was to begin in March 2010, but drilling still delayed as of September 2011. ("China Curbs Iran	CNPC (China)	$4.7 billion	
	Energy Work," Reuters, September 2, 2011)			
Totals: $41 billion investment				
Other Pending/Preliminary Deals				
North Pars Gas Field (offshore gas). Includes gas purchases (December 2006)		China National Offshore Oil Co.	$16 billion	3.6 billion cfd
Work crews reportedly pulled from the project in early-mid 2011. ("China Curbs Iran Energy Work"Reuters, September 2, 2011)				
Phase 13, 14—South Pars (gas); (Feb. 2007). Deadline to finalize as May 20, 2009, apparently		Royal Dutch Shell, Repsol (Spain)	$4.3 billion	?

Date	Field/Project	Company(ies)/Status (If Known)	Value	Output/Goal
not met; firms submitted revised proposals to Iran inJune 2009. (http://www.rigzone.com/news/ article.asp?a_id=77040&hmpn=1.) State Department said on September 30, 2010, that Royal Dutch Shell and Repsol have ended negotiations with Iran and will not pursue this project any further				
Phase 22, 23, 24—South Pars (gas), incl. transport Iranian gas to Turkey, and on to Europe and building three power plants in Iran. Initialed July 2007; not finalized to date.		Turkish Petroleum Company (TPAO)	$12. billion	2 billion cfd
Iran's Kish gas field (April 2008) Includes pipeline from Iran to Oman (http://www.presstv.ir/detail.aspx?id=112062& sectionid=351020103.)		Oman (co-financing of project)	$7 billion	1 billion cfd
Phase 12 South Pars (gas)—part 1. Incl. LNG terminal construction and Farzad-B natural gas bloc (March 2009). Financing stalled due to sanctions; Tehran gave ONGC and Hinduja until January 31, 2011, to line up financing or the bid will be considered abandoned.		Taken over by Indian firms (ONGC, Oil India Ltd., Hinduja, Petronet in 2007). May also involve Sonanagol (Angola) and PDVSA(Venezuela)	$8 billion from Indian firms/$1.5 billion Sonangol/$ 780 million PDVSA	20 million tonnes of LNG annually by 2012
Abadan refinery Upgrade and expansion; building a new refinery at Hormuz on the Persian Gulf coast (August 2009)		Sinopec	up to $6 billion if new refinery is built	

Sources: As noted in table, as well as CRS conversations with officials of the State Department Bureau of Economics, and officials of embassies of the parent government of some of the listed companies (2005-2009). Some information comes: March 2010 GAO report, "Firms Reported in Open Sources as Having Commercial Activity in Iran's Oil, Gas, and Petrochemical Sectors." GAO-10-515R Iran's Oil, Gas, and Petrochemical Sectors. http://www.gao.gov /new.items/d10515r.pdf. The GAO report lists 41 firms with "commercial activity in Iran's energy sector; several of the listed agreements do not appear to constitute "investment," as defined in ISA. That report was updated on August 3, 2011, in GAO-11-855R. http://www.gao.gov/new.items/ d11855r .pdf.

Note: CRS has neither the mandate, the authority, nor the means to determine which of these projects, if any, might constitute a violation of the Iran Sanctions Act. CRS has no way to confirm the precise status of any of the announced investments, and some investments may have been resold to other firms or terms altered since agreement. In virtually all cases, such investments and contracts represent private agreements between Iran and its instruments and the investing firms, and firms are not necessarily required to confirm or publicly release the terms of their arrangements with Iran. Reported $20 million+ investments in oil and gas fields, refinery upgrades, and major project leadership are included in this table. Responsibility for a project to develop Iran's energy sector is part of ISA investment definition.

Effect on Gasoline Availability and Importation

In March 2010, well before the enactment of CISADA on July 1, 2010, several gas suppliers to Iran, anticipating this legislation, announced that they had stopped or would stop supplying gasoline to Iran.56 Others have ceased since the enactment of CISADA.

Some observers say that gasoline deliveries to Iran fell from about 120,000 barrels per day before CISADA to about 30,000 barrels per day immediately thereafter,57 although importation had recovered somewhat to about 80,000 barrels per day by September 2011.

That suggests that Iran has lined up additional supplies from those still willing to do business with Iran. As noted in a New York Times report of March 7, 2010,[58] and a Government Accountability Office study released September 3, 2010,[59] some firms that have supplied Iran have received U.S. credit guarantees or contracts.

The main suppliers to Iran over the past few years, and the GAO-reported status of their sales to Iran are listed below (with the caveat that some reports say that partners or affiliates of these firms may still sell to Iran in cases where the corporate headquarters have announced a halt):

- Vitol of Switzerland (notified GAO it stopped selling to Iran in early 2010);
- Trafigura of Switzerland (notified GAO it stopped selling to Iran in November 2009);
- Glencore of Switzerland (notified GAO it stopped selling in September 2009);
- Total of France (notified GAO it stopped sales to Iran in May 2010);
- Reliance Industries of India (notified GAO it stopped sales to Iran in May 2009). Reliance has also told press outlets on April 1, 2010, that it would not import Iranian crude oil in 2010;
- Petronas of Malaysia (said on April 15, 2010, it had stopped sales to Iran);[60]
- Lukoil of Russia (reportedly to have ended sales to Iran in in April 2010,[61] although some reports continue that Lukoil affiliates are supplying Iran);
- Royal Dutch Shell of the Netherlands (notified GAO it stopped sales in October 2009);
- Kuwait's Independent Petroleum Group told U.S. officials it is no longer selling gasoline to Iran, as of September 2010;[62]

- Tupras of Turkey (according to the State Department on May 24, 2011);
- British Petroleum of United Kingdom, Shell, Q8, Total, and OMV are no longer selling aviation fuel to Iran Air, according to U.S. State Department officials on May 24, 2011;
- A UAE firm, Golden Crown Petroleum FZE, told the author in April 2011 that, as of June 29, 2010, it no longer leases vessels for the purpose of shipping petroleum products from or through Iran;
- Munich Re, Allianz, Hannover Re (Germany) were providing insurance and reinsurance for gasoline shipments to Iran. However, they reportedly have exited the market for insuring gasoline shipments for Iran;[63]
- Lloyd's (Britain). The major insurer had been the main company insuring Iranian gas (and other) shipping, but reportedly has ended that business as of July 2010 According to the State Department, key shipping associations have created clauses in their contracts that enable ship owners to refuse to deliver gasoline to Iran;
- The State Department reported on September 30, 2010, that Hong Kong company NYK Line Ltd. had ended shipping business with Iran (on any goods, not just gasoline);
- According to the State Department on May 24, 2011, Linde of Germany has said it had stopped supplying gas liquefaction technology to Iran, contributing to Iran's decision to suspend its LNG program.

Firms Believed to Still Be Supplying Gasoline or Related Equipment

- The firms sanctioned by the administration on May 24, 2011 (discussed above): PCCI (Jersey/Iran); Royal Oyster Group (UAE); Speedy Ship (UAE/Iran); Tanker Pacific (Singapore); Ofer Brothers Group (Israel); Associated Shipbroking (Monaco); and Petroleos de Venezuela (Venezuela);
- Zhuhai Zhenrong, Unipec, and China Oil of China are said by GAO to still be selling to Iran and have not denied continuing sales to the GAO;
- Emirates National Oil Company of UAE was reported by GAO to still be selling to Iran;

- Hin Leong Trading of Singapore was reported by GAO to still be selling gasoline to Iran;
- Some refiners in Bahrain reportedly may still be selling gasoline to Iran.

Despite the reduction in gasoline sales to Iran, Iranian officials have largely coped with the reduction in gasoline imports. The phaseout of gasoline subsidies discussed above has already reportedly begun to reduce demand for gasoline.

Iran has also increased domestic production by converting at least two petrochemical plants to gasoline production, through a generally inferior process that initially produces benzene.

The gasoline produced reportedly has led to a large increase in air pollution in Tehran, which was expected. Iran also says it has accelerated renovations and other improvements to existing gasoline refineries, allocating $2.2 billion for that purpose.

Even before the subsidy reduction, there had not been gasoline shortages or gasoline rationing, although some Iranian oppositionists have reported otherwise.

Building new refining capacity appears to be Iran's long term effort to reduce its vulnerability to gasoline supply reductions. Iran's deputy oil minister said in July 2010 Iran would try to invest $46 billion to upgrade its nine refineries and build seven new ones, a far larger amount than Iran had previously allocated to oil refining capacity.

ADDITIONAL SANCTIONS: POSSIBLE LEGISLATION, ADMINISTRATIVE, AND MULTILATERAL ACTION

Some in the 112th Congress believe that the cumulative effect ofUS and international sanctions—even after the U.S. British, and Canadian steps taken on November 21, 2011—remain insufficient to accomplish key U.S. policy goals toward Iran, and are advocating further steps. Still, the administration is said to prefer taking its own action rather than be bound by specific congressional requirements, and in testimony before the Senate Foreign Relations Committee on December 1, 2011, Treasury Undersecretary Cohen expressed concern about congressional initiatives that could raise world oil prices or cause U.S. partners to distance themselves from the joint effort to isolate Iran.

A House bill, H.R. 1905, the "Iran Threat Reduction Act of 2011" was marked up by the House Foreign Affairs Committee on November 2, 2011, along with H.R. 2105. As amended on November 2, H.R. 1905, contains language restating provisions of ISA and would:

- Add two sanctions to the available ISA menu: a ban on visas for the principal officers or controlling shareholders of sanctioned firms (and their subsidiaries, parents, and affiliates); and apply any ISA sanction to the principal officers of a sanctioned firm.
- Require the president to impose at least six out of the expanded ISA menu of 11 available sanctions on any sanctioned firm.
- Make subject to ISA sanctions (majority of the menu) any firm that helps Iran issue sovereign debt.
- Prohibit U.S. persons, subject to penalty, from conducting any business with the Revolutionary Guard of its affiliated entities, or with any foreign firm that conducts such banned transactions with the Revolutionary Guard or its affiliates.
- Ban commerce between Iran and subsidiaries of U.S. firms, in cases where the subsidiary is controlled or more than 50% owned by the parent firm.
- Ban previously permissible licensing of the sale to Iran of U.S. equipment to provide for the safe operation of Iran's civilian aircraft fleet.
- State that it is U.S. policy to support those in Iran seeking democracy, and rquire an administration submission to Congress of a comprehensive strategy to help the Iranian people circumvent regime censorship and monitoring of their use of the Internet or other media.
- Require an administration report listing all persons who are members of named Iranian government institutions, including high ranking Revolutionary Guard officers—and ban visas for the named individuals.
- Ban contact between any U.S. official and any Iranian official who poses a threat to the United States or is affiliated with terrorist organizations.
- Contain elements similar to H.R. 740 on Securities and Exchange Commission (SEC) disclosures, discussed further below.

- Sanction Iran's Central Bank if the president determines that it helped Iran acquire WMD or facilitated transactions for the Revolutionary Guard or for entities sanctioned by the United States.
- Set as U.S. policy to press Iraq not to close Camp Ashraf, an encampment in Iraq which houses about 3,300 Iranian oppositionists, unless the residents can be resettled.

No date for a floor vote on H.R. 1905 has been announced. However some observers say that the House might act on it before the end of 2011.

A Senate bill that focuses primarily on economic sanctions and proliferation sanctions is S. 1048, introduced May 23, 2011, and titled the "Iran, North Korea, and Syria Sanctions Consolidation Act of 2011." (As noted above, a companion measure, H.R. 2105, was marked up on November 2, 2011.) Among other provisions, S.1048:

- States (Section 101) that it is the policy of the United States to prevent Iran from acquiring a nuclear weapons capability.
- Primarily targets affiliates of the Revolutionary Guard for sanctions, and expands the list of sanctions (adding a ban on financing, aid, or investment) to be imposed on violators named under the Iran, Syria, North Korea Non-Proliferation Act, discussed above.
- Like H.R. 1905, subjects to ISA sanctions purchases of Iranian oil or gas in which the IRGC or its affiliates are involved. Unlike H.R. 1905, S. 1048 (Section 123) also mandates sanctions (ban on U.S. government contracts and ban on imports to the United States) of any entity determined to have conducted any commercial or financial transaction with the IRGC or its affiliates.
- Would sanction foreign firms that participate in energy-related joint ventures with Iran outside Iranian territory.
- Would prohibit ships to put into port in the United States if the vessel entered a port in Iran, North Korea, or Syria any time 180 days prior.
- Like H.R. 1905, would deny visas to senior officials of Iran, but extends that to North Korea and Syria, and does not define specific government agencies in Iran whose members shall be named by the administration.
- Provides for sanctions against any person determined to be providing or acquiring militarily useful equipment to/from Iran, North Korea, or Syria.

- Contains Iran human rights-related and SEC disclosure provisions similar to bills discussed below.

Sanctioning Iran's Central Bank

As demonstrated by other pending legislation, there appears to be growing support in Congress to sanction Iran's Central Bank. Currently, there are no mandatory sanctions against Iran's Central Bank (Bank Markazi) itself, although certain activities involving the Bank are potentially sanctionable, as discussed above. In addition, as noted, on November 21, the Treasury Department designated all of Iran's financial sector, including the Central Bank (and all Iranian banks) as "money laundering entities" for Iran-related transactions under Section 311 of the USA Patriot Act. However, the Treasury Department has not imposed any specific sanctions against Iran's Central Bank for its efforts, discussed in numerous accounts, to help other Iranian banks circumvent the U.S. and U.N. banking pressure. If there were evidence to support such judgments, Treasury could potentially designate it as a proliferation entity under Executive order 13382 or a terrorism supporting entity under Executive Order 13224.

Some in Congress see sanctioning the Central Bank as an effective additional option to pressure Iran and were not satisfied by the November 21 Treasury designation of the Iranian financial sector as a money laundering entity. The amendment to H.R. 1905 that appears likely, if passed and signed, to trigger sanctions against the Central Bank is discussed above. A separate effort was introduced as an amendment to a FY2012 national defense authorization bill (S.1867). Introduced by Senators Mark Kirk and Robert Menendez, the amendment would require the president to prevent a foreign bank from opening an account in the United States if that bank processes payments for oil (and not applicable to other transactions) through Iran's Central Bank. The amendment provides for a renewable waiver of 120 days duration if the president determines that doing so is in the national interest. On December 1, 2011, the amendment passed 100-0, although administration opposition could lead to modifications to the provision in further legislative action. The recent congressional initiatives built on an August 9, 2011, a letter signed by 92 Senators was sent to President Obama urging "a comprehensive strategy to pressure Iran's financial system by imposing sanctions" on the Central Bank of Iran.

Some in Congress appeared to believe that the administration supports sanctioning the Central Bank. In testimony before several congressional committees in October 2011, Treasury Undersecretary Cohen had stated that the administration is considering sanctioning the Central Bank if the United States is able to get broad international acceptance for doing so. administration officials had also noted that sanctioning a Central Bank of a country, although sensitive, is not unprecedented – the central banks of Sudan and Libya had been sanctioned in the past. However, testimony by Undersecretary Cohen before the Senate Foreign Relations Committee on December 2, 2011, but before the vote on the Kirk-Menendez amendment, stated “strong opposition” to the amendment because it could lead to a rise in oil prices that would actually benefit Iran. Others argue that administration opposition might have been mitigated by the inclusion in the amendment of the waiver provision.

The administration opposition is in part because several European countries reportedly have opposed such a sanction as an extreme step. If the Central Bank of Iran were cut off from the international banking system, it is possible that all mechanisms for paying Iran for crude oil would be shut down. That raises the potential for Iran to stop exporting oil, an action that would undoubtedly cause a significant rise in world oil prices. Alternatively, Iran might accept payment in goods or services, or in currencies that are non-convertible or difficult to convert.

In addition, one of the Central Bank’s roles is to keep Iran’s currency, the rial, stable. It does so by using hard currency to buy rials to raise the currency value, or to sell rials to bring the value down. An unstable currency could harm Iran’s ability to import some needed foodstuffs and medical products, according to those opposing that sanction. However, suggesting possibly eroding European opposition to sanctioning the Central Bank, Resolution 1929 references the need for vigilance in dealing with the Bank, but did not mandate any new sanctions against it. In addition, the EU discussions of a voluntary embargo on purchases of Iranian oil could also lead to an acceptance of U.S. sanctions against Iran’s Central Bank.

Other Trends in the 112th Congress

Another apparent trend in the 112th Congress, based on introduced legislation, is to expand the sanctioning of Iranians named as human rights abusers. This builds on the human rights provisions of CISADA and the earlier Iran Freedom Support Act. In particular, the Iran Human Rights and Democracy Promotion Act of 2011 (S. 879 and H.R. 1714) would: make mandatory investigations of Iranian human rights abusers; sanction the sale to Iran of equipment that could be used to suppress demonstrations; reauthorize the Iran Freedom Support Act (see below); and create a “Special Representative” position at the Department of State to focus on highlighting

Iran's human rights abuses and coordinate U.S. and international responses. As noted, portions of H.R. 1905 and S. 1048, which mainly focus on economic sanctions, also contain measures to further penalize Iranian human rights abusers or otherwise promote Internet freedom and democracy in Iran.

Other economic sanctions-related measures introduced in the 112th Congress include S. 366 and H.R. 740. These bills would require firms to declare in their required filings with the Securities and Exchange Commission whether that firm had undertaken activity that could violate ISA, CISADA, or executive orders (13224 or 13382) and regulations that bar dealings with designated Iranian entities.

Possible Additional Multilateral Sanctions

Although there do not appear to be active discussions among the P5+1 on specific new United Nations actions to pressure Iran, there are a number of other possible sanctions that might receive consideration – either in a multilateral framework or for U.S. unilateral action targeting foreign firms and entities.

Comprehensive Oil Embargo

Most experts believe that the most effective sanction would be a mandated, worldwide embargo on the purchase of Iranian crude oil. There are no indications that such a step is to be proposed at the United Nations in the near term or that doing so would achieve consensus. However, as noted above, a voluntary ban on importing Iranian oil is under consideration by the EU, at French and British urging. Were such a voluntary ban to be adopted, there would likely be pressure on Japan and South Korea to follow suit. That could potentially leave China alone as a very large buyer of Iranian oil, conceivably enabling China to force down the price it pays for Iranian oil. However, some might argue that if this trend turned into a comprehensive, worldwide voluntary embargo, world oil prices might rise significantly. Ideas to mitigate such effects include a delay period to allow for re-adjustment of the oil market.

A U.S. unilateral move to compel others to cease purchasing Iranian oil does not appear under consideration. Short of imposing a military quarantine on Iran, the United States does not have the ability, by itself, to prevent Iran from exporting oil. However, as in the case of the Iran Sanctions Act, U.S. law could be used to force international energy firms to choose between buying Iranian oil or continuing their "business as usual" in the very large U.S. market. This step does not appear under consideration in the administration.

Some in Congress do want to compel other countries to stop buying Iranian oil or to limit such purchases. In the 111th Congress, Representative Sherman introduced H.R. 6296, which, in Section 202, would amend ISA to make sanctionable "long term agreements" to buy oil from Iran—agreements that would involve large, up-front payments to Iran for purchases of oil over a long period of time. A provision of that bill would have extended ISA sanctionability to any energy project conducted with NIOC, anywhere in the world. An amended version of the bill was introduced in the 112th Congress (H.R. 1655, introduced April 15, 2011).

Iran "Oil-Free Zone"

There reportedly has been discussion among experts of closing the loophole in the U.S. trade ban under which Iranian crude oil, when mixed with other countries' oils at foreign refineries in Europe and elsewhere, can be imported as refined product. The basis of the proposal, outlined by a think-tank called the Foundation of Defense of Democracies, is that restricting Iranian oil to use by only a limited number of refineries would force down the price received by Iran for its oil, although without raising the world price of oil significantly, if at all.

Other Possibilities

Other possible international steps would likely have less of an adverse economic effect on the countries imposing those sanctions on Iran but would, if enacted in a U.N.

Security Council resolution, be binding on U.N. member states and presumably have greater effect than would such steps by the United States alone or in concert with its allies.

- *Mandating Reductions in Diplomatic Exchanges with Iran or Prohibiting Travel by Iranian Officials.* Some have suggested a worldwide ban on travel to Iranian civilian officials, such as those involved in suppressing democracy activists. Some have called on countries to reduce their diplomatic presence in Iran, or to expel some Iranian diplomats from Iranian embassies in their territories.
- However, the EU came one steps closer to this option after the November 29 attack on the British Embassy in Tehran: Britain closed the Iranian embassy in Britain, and Norway, France, Germany, and the Netherlands withdrew their ambassadors. The EU, as noted, on December 1 named numerous Iranian persons as subject to a visa ban.

- *Barring Iran from International Sporting Events.* A further option is to limit sports or cultural exchanges with Iran, such as Iran's participation in the World Cup soccer tournament. However, many experts oppose using sporting events to accomplish political goals.
- *Banning Passenger Flights to and from Iran.* Bans on flights to and from Libya were imposed on that country in response to the finding that its agents were responsible for the December 21, 1988, bombing of Pan Am 103 (now lifted). There are no indications that a passenger aircraft flight ban is under consideration among the P5+1.
- *A Ban on Exports to Iran of Refined Oil Products and Energy Equipment and Services.* As noted, the EU sanctions formalized July 27, 2010, did not ban sales of gasoline but did ban the sale to Iran of equipment or services for Iran's energy sector (refineries as well as exploration and drilling). Another possibility would be to make such a general ban on sales of energy equipment or services universal in a new U.N. resolution. U.N. sanctions against Libya for the Pan Am 103 bombing banned the sale of energy equipment to Libya.
- *Limiting Lending to Iran by International Financial Institutions.* Resolution 1747 calls for restraint on but does not outright ban international lending to Iran. An option is to make a ban on such lending mandatory.
- *Banning Trade Financing or Official Insurance for Trade Financing.* Another option is to mandate a ban on official trade credit guarantees. This was not made mandatory by Resolution 1929, but several countries imposed this sanction (as far as most trade financing) subsequently. In discussions that led to Resolution 1929, a ban on investment in Iranian bonds reportedly was considered but deleted to attract China and Russia's support.
- Banning Worldwide Investment in Iran's Energy Sector. This option would represent an "internationalization" of the U.S. "Iran Sanctions Act." Such a step is authorized, not mandated, by Resolution 1929, and a growing number of countries have used that authority to impose these sanctions on Iran.
- Restricting Operations of and Insurance for Iranian Shipping. One option, reportedly long under consideration, has been to ban the provision of insurance, or reinsurance, for any shipping to Iran. A call for restraint is in Resolution 1929, but is not mandatory. The EU and other national measures announced.subsequently did include this

sanction (IRISL) to operate. (The United States has imposed sanctions on IRISL.)

- Imposing a Worldwide Ban on Sales of Arms to Iran. Resolution 1929 imposes a ban on sales of major weapons systems to Iran, but another option is to extend that ban to all lethal equipment.

Table 6. Entities Sanctioned Under U.N. Resolutions and U.S. Laws and Executive Orders (Persons listed are identified by the positions they held when designated; some have since changed)

Entities Named for Sanctions under Resolution 1737

Atomic Energy Organization of Iran (AEIO) Mesbah Energy Company (Arak supplier)
Kalaye Electric (Natanz supplier))
Pars Trash Company (centrifuge program) Farayand Technique (centrifuge program)
Defense Industries Organization (DIO)
7th of Tir (DIO subordinate)
Shahid Hemmat Industrial Group (SHIG)—missile program
Shahid Bagheri Industrial Group (SBIG)—missile program
Fajr Industrial Group (missile program)
Mohammad Qanadi, AEIO Vice President
Behman Asgarpour (Arak manager)
Ehsan Monajemi (Natanz construction manager)
Jafar Mohammadi (Adviser to AEIO)
Gen. Hosein Salimi (Commander, IRGC Air Force)
Dawood Agha Jani (Natanz official)
Ali Hajinia Leilabadi (director of Mesbah Energy)
Lt. Gen. Mohammad Mehdi Nejad Nouri (Malak Ashtar University of Defence Technology rector)
Bahmanyar Morteza Bahmanyar (AIO official)
Reza Gholi Esmaeli (AIO official)
Ahmad Vahid Dastjerdi (head of Aerospace Industries Org., AIO)
Maj. Gen. Yahya Rahim Safavi (Commander in Chief, IRGC)

Entities/Persons Added by Resolution 1747

Ammunition and Metallurgy Industries Group (controls 7th of Tir)
archinChemical Industries (branch of DIO)
Karaj Nuclear Research Center
Novin Energy Company
Cruise Missile Industry Group
Sanam Industrial Group (subordinate to AIO)
Ya Mahdi Industries Group
Kavoshyar Company (subsidiary of AEIO)
Sho'a Aviation (produces IRGC light aircraft for asymmetric warfare)
Bank Sepah (funds AIO and subordinate entities)
Esfahan Nuclear Fuel Research and Production Center and Esfahan Nuclear Technology Center
Qods Aeronautics Industries (produces UAV's, para-gliders for IRGC asymmetric warfare)
Pars Aviation Services Company (maintains IRGC Air Force equipment)
Gen. Mohammad Baqr Zolqadr (IRGC officer serving as deputy Interior Minister

Brig. Gen. Qasem Soleimani (Qods Force commander)
Fereidoun Abbasi-Davani (senior defense scientist)
Mohasen Fakrizadeh-Mahabai (defense scientist)
Seyed Jaber Safdari (Natanz manager)
Mohsen Hojati (head of Fajr Industrial Group)
Ahmad Derakshandeh (head of Bank Sepah)
Brig. Gen. Mohammad Reza Zahedi (IRGC ground forces commander)
Amir Rahimi (head of Esfahan nuclear facilities)
Mehrdada Akhlaghi Ketabachi (head of SBIG)
Naser Maleki (head of SHIG)
Brig. Gen. Morteza Reza'i (Deputy commander-in-chief, IRGC)
Vice Admiral Ali Akbar Ahmadiyan (chief of IRGC Joint Staff)
Brig. Gen. Mohammad Hejazi (Basij commander)

Entities Added by Resolution 1803

Thirteen Iranians named in Annex 1 to Resolution 1803; all reputedly involved in various aspects of nuclear program. Bans travel for five named Iranians.
Electro Sanam Co.
Abzar Boresh Kaveh Co. (centrifuge production)
Barzaganin Tejaral Tavanmad Saccal
Jabber Ibn Hayan
Khorasan Metallurgy Industries
Niru Battery Manufacturing Co. (Makes batteries for Iranian military and missile systems)
Ettehad Technical Group (AIO front co.)
Industrial Factories of Precision
Joza Industrial Co.
Pshgam (Pioneer) Energy Industries
Tamas Co. (involved in uranium enrichment)
Safety Equipment Procurement (AIO front, involved in missiles)

Entities Added by Resolution 1929

Over 40 entities added; makes mandatory a previously nonbinding travel ban on most named Iranians of previous resolutions.
Adds one individual banned for travel—AEIO head Javad Rahiqi
Amin Industrial Complex
Armament Industries Group
Defense Technology and Science Research Center (owned or controlled by Ministry of Defense).
Doostan International Company
Farasakht Industries
First East Export Bank, PLC (only bank added by Resolution 1929)
Kaveh Cutting Tools Company
M. Babaie Industries
Malek Ashtar University (subordinate of Defense Technology and Science Research Center, above)
Ministry of Defense Logistics Export (sells Iranian made arms to customers worldwide)
Mizan Machinery Manufacturing
Modern Industries Technique Company
Nuclear Research Center for Agriculture and Medicine (research component of the AEIO)
Pejman Industrial Services Corp.
Sabalan Company
Sahand Aluminum Parts Industrial Company
Shahid Karrazi Industries
Shahid Sattari Industries
Shahid Sayyade Shirazi Industries (acts on behalf of the DIO)
Special Industries Group (another subordinate of DIO)

Table 6. (Continued)

Tiz Pars (cover name for SHIG)
Yazd Metallurgy Industries
The following are Revolutionary Guard affiliated firms, several are subsidiaries of Khatam ol-Anbiya, the main Guard construction affiliate:
Fater Institute
Garaghe Sazendegi Ghaem
Gorb Karbala
Gorb Nooh
Hara Company
Imensazan Consultant Engineers Institute
Khatam ol-Anbiya
Makin
Omran Sahel
Oriental Oil Kish
Rah Sahel
Rahab Engineering Institute
Sahel Consultant Engineers
Sepanir
Sepasad Engineering Company
The following are entities owned or controlled by Islamic Republic of Iran Shipping Lines (IRISL):
Irano Hind Shipping Company
IRISL Benelux
South Shipping Line Iran

Entities Designated Under U.S. Executive Order 13382 (many designations coincident with designations under U.N. resolutions)

Entity	Date Named
Shahid Hemmat Industrial Group (Iran)	June 2005, September 2007
Shahid Bakeri Industrial Group (Iran)	June 2005, February 2009
Atomic Energy Organization of Iran	June 2005
Novin Energy Company (Iran)	January 2006
Mesbah Energy Company (Iran)	January 2006
Four Chinese entities: Beijing Alite Technologies, LIMMT Economic and Trading Company, China Great Wall Industry Corp, and China National Precision Machinery Import/Export Corp.	June 2006
Sanam Industrial Group (Iran)	July 2006
Ya Mahdi Industries Group (Iran)	July 2006
Bank Sepah (Iran)	January 2007
Defense Industries Organization (Iran)	March 2007
Pars Trash (Iran, nuclear program)	June 2007
Farayand Technique (Iran, nuclear program)	June 2007
Fajr Industries Group (Iran, missile program)	June 2007
Mizan Machine Manufacturing Group (Iran, missile prog.)	June 2007
Aerospace Industries Organization (AIO) (Iran)	September 2007
Korea Mining and Development Corp. (N. Korea)	September 2007
Islamic Revolutionary Guard Corps (IRGC)	October 21, 2007
Ministry of Defense and Armed Forces Logistics	October 21, 2007
Bank Melli (Iran's largest bank, widely used by Guard); Bank Melli Iran Zao (Moscow); Melli Bank PC (U.K.)	October 21, 2007
Bank Kargoshaee	October 21, 2007

Arian Bank (joint venture between Melli and Bank Saderat). Based in Afghanistan	October 21, 2007
Entity	Date Named
Bank Mellat (provides banking services to Iran's nuclear sector); Mellat Bank SB CJSC (Armenia). Reportedly has $1.4 billion in assets in UAE	October 21, 2007
Persia International Bank PLC (U.K.)	October 21, 2007
Khatam ol Anbiya Gharargah Sazendegi Nooh (main IRGC construction and contracting arm, with $7 billion in oil, gas deals)	October 21, 2007
Oriental Oil Kish (Iranian oil exploration firm)	October 21, 2007
Ghorb Karbala; Ghorb Nooh (synonymous with Khatam ol Anbiya)	October 21, 2007
Sepasad Engineering Company (Guard construction affiliate)	October 21, 2007
Omran Sahel (Guard construction affiliate)	October 21, 2007
Sahel Consultant Engineering (Guard construction affiliate)	October 21, 2007
Hara Company	October 21, 2007
Gharargahe Sazandegi Ghaem	October 21, 2007
Bahmanyar Morteza Bahmanyar (AIO, Iran missile official, see above under Resolution 1737)	October 21, 2007
Ahmad Vahid Dastjerdi (AIO head, Iran missile program)	October 21, 2007
Reza Gholi Esmaeli (AIO, see under Resolution 1737)	October 21, 2007
Morteza Reza'i (deputy commander, IRGC) See also Resolution 1747	October 21, 2007
Mohammad Hejazi (Basij commander). Also, Resolution 1747	October 21, 2007
Ali Akbar Ahmadian (Chief of IRGC Joint Staff). Resolution 1747	October 21, 2007
Hosein Salimi (IRGC Air Force commander). Resolution 1737	October 21, 2007
Qasem Soleimani (Qods Force commander). Resolution 1747	October 21, 2007
Future Bank (Bahrain-based but allegedly controlled by Bank Melli)	March 12, 2008
Yahya Rahim Safavi (former IRGC Commander in Chief	July 8, 2008
Mohsen Fakrizadeh-Mahabadi (senior Defense Ministry scientist)	July 8, 2008
Dawood Agha-Jani (head of Natanz enrichment site)	July 8, 2008
Mohsen Hojati (head of Fajr Industries, involved in missile program)	July 8, 2008
Mehrdada Akhlaghi Ketabachi (heads Shahid Bakeri Industrial Group)	July 8, 2008
Naser Maliki (heads Shahid Hemmat Industrial Group)	July 8, 2008
Tamas Company (involved in uranium enrichment)	July 8, 2008
Shahid Sattari Industries (makes equipment for Shahid Bakeri)	July 8, 2008
7th of Tir (involved in developing centrifuge technology)	July 8, 2008
Ammunition and Metallurgy Industries Group (partner of 7th of Tir)	July 8, 2008
Parchin Chemical Industries (deals in chemicals used in ballistic missile programs)	July 8, 2008
Karaj Nuclear Research Center	August 12, 2008
Esfahan Nuclear Fuel Research and Production Center (NFRPC)	August 12, 2008
Jabber Ibn Hayyan (reports to Atomic Energy Org. of Iran, AEIO)	August 12, 2008
Safety Equipment Procurement Company	August 12, 2008
Joza Industrial Company (front company for Shahid Hemmat Industrial Group, SHIG)	August 12, 2008
Islamic Republic of Iran Shipping Lines (IRISL) and 18 affiliates, including Val Fajr 8; Kazar; Irinvestship; Shipping Computer Services; Iran o Misr Shipping; Iran o Hind; IRISL Marine Services; Iriatal Shipping; South Shipping; IRISL Multimodal; Oasis; IRISL Europe; IRISL Benelux; IRISL China; Asia Marine Network; CISCO Shipping; and IRISL Malta	September 10, 2008

Table 6. (Continued)

Entity	Date Named
Firms affiliated to the Ministry of Defense, including Armament Industries Group; Farasakht Industries; Iran Aircraft Manufacturing Industrial Co.; Iran Communications Industries; Iran Electronics Industries; and Shiraz Electronics Industries	September 17, 2008
Export Development Bank of Iran. Provides financial services to Iran's Ministry of Defense and Armed Forces Logistics	October 22, 2008
Banco Internacional de Desarollo, C.A., Venezuelan-based Iranian bank, sanctioned as an affiliate of the Export Development Bank.	
Assa Corporation (alleged front for Bank Melli involved in managing property in New York City on behalf of Iran)	December 17, 2008
11 Entities Tied to Bank Melli: Bank Melli Iran Investment (BMIIC); Bank Melli Printing and Publishing; Melli Investment Holding; Mehr Cayman Ltd.; Cement Investment and Development; Mazandaran Cement Co.; Shomal Cement; Mazandaran Textile; Melli Agrochemical; First Persian Equity Fund; BMIIC Intel. General Trading	March 3, 2009
IRGC General Rostam Qasemi, head of Khatem ol-Anbiya Construction Headquarters (key corporate arm of the IRGC)	February 10, 2010 (see also October 21, 2007)
Fater Engineering Institute (linked to Khatem ol-Anbiya)	February 10, 2010
Imensazen Consultant Engineers Institute (linked to Khatem ol-Anbiya)	February 10, 2010
Makin Institute (linked to Khatem ol-Anbiya)	February 10, 2010
Rahab Institute (linked to Khatem on-Anbiya)	February 10, 2010

Entities sanctioned on June 16, 2010

- Post Bank of Iran
- IRGC Air Force
- IRGC Missile Command
- Rah Sahel and Sepanir Oil and Gas Engineering (for ties to Khatem ol-Anibya IRGC construction affiliate)
- Mohammad Ali Jafari—IRGC Commander-in-Chief since September 2007
- Mohammad Reza Naqdi—Head of the IRGC's Basij militia force that suppresses dissent (since October 2009)
- Ahmad Vahedi—Defense Minister
- javedan Mehr Toos, Javad Karimi Sabet (procurement brokers or atomic energy managers)
- Naval Defense Missile Industry Group (controlled by the Aircraft Industries Org that manages Iran's missile programs)
- Five front companies for IRISL: Hafiz Darya Shipping Co.; Soroush Sarzamin Asatir Ship Management Co.; Safiran Payam Darya;

and Hong Kong-based Seibow Limited and Seibow Logistics.
Also identified on June 16 were 27 vessels linked to IRISKL and 71 new names of already designated IRISL ships.
Several Iranian entities were also designated as owned or controlled by Iran for purposes of the ban on U.S. trade with Iran.
Entities sanctioned on November 30, 2010

- Pearl Energy Company (formed by First East Export Bank , a subsidiary of Bank Mellat
- Pearl Energy Services, SA
- Ali Afzali (high official of First East Export Bank)

- IRISL front companies: Ashtead Shipping, Byfleet Shipping, Cobham Shipping, Dorking Shipping, Effingham Shipping, Farnham Shipping, Gomshall Shipping, and Horsham Shipping (all located in the Isle of Man).
- IRISL and affiliate officials: Mohammad Hosein Dajmar, Gholamhossein Golpavar, Hassan Jalil Zadeh, and Mohammad Haji Pajand.

Entities sanctioned on December 21, 2010:
- Bonyad (foundation) Taavon Sepah, for providing services to the IRGC
- Ansar Bank (for providing financial services to the IRGC)
- Mehr Bank (same justification as above)
- Moallem Insurance Company (for providing marine insurance to IRISL, Islamic Republic of Iran Shipping Lines)

Bank of Industry and Mine (BIM)	May 17, 2011
- Tidewater Middle East Company	June 23, 2011
- Iran Air	
- Mehr-e Eqtesad Iranian Investment Co.	

Entities Sanctioned Under Executive Order 13224 (Terrorism Entities)

Qods Force	October 21, 2007
Bank Saderat (allegedly used to funnel Iranian money to Hezbollah, Hamas, PIJ, and other Iranian supported terrorist groups)	October 21, 2007
Al Qaeda Operatives in Iran: Saad bin Laden; Mustafa Hamid; Muhammad Rab'a al-Bahtiyti; Alis Saleh Husain	January 16, 2009
Qods Force senior officers: Hushang Allahdad, Hossein Musavi,Hasan Mortezavi, and Mohammad Reza Zahedi	August 3, 2010
Iranian Committee for the Reconstruction of Lebanon, and its director Hesam Khoshnevis, for supporting Lebanese Hizballah	August 3, 2010
Imam Khomeini Relief Committee Lebanon branch, and its director Ali Zuraik, for providing support to Hizballah	August 3, 2010
Razi Musavi, a Syrian based Iranian official allegedly providing support to Hizballah	August 3, 2010
Liner Transport Kish (for providing shipping services to transport weapons to Lebanese Hizballah)	December 21, 2010
For alleged plot against Saudi Ambassador to the U.S.: Qasem Soleimani (Qods Force commander) Hamid Abdollahi (Qods force) Abdul Reza Shahlai (Qods Force) Ali Gholam Shakuri (Qods Force) Manssor Arbabsiar (alleged plotter)	October 11, 2011
Mahan Air (for transportation services to Qods Force)	October 12, 2011

Entities Sanctioned Under the Iran North Korea Syria Non-Proliferation Act or Executive Order 12938

The designations are under the Iran, North Korea, Syria Non-Proliferation Act (INKSNA) unless specified. These designations expire after two years, unless re-designated

Baltic State Technical University and Glavkosmos, both of Russia	July 30, 1998 (E.O. 12938). Both removed in 2010—Baltic on Jan. 29, 2010, and Glavkosmos on March 4, 2010
D. Mendeleyev University of Chemical Technology of Russia and Moscow Aviation Institute	January 8, 1999 (E.O. 12938). Both removed on May 21, 2010

Table 6. (Continued)

Norinco (China). For alleged missile technology sale to Iran.	May 2003
Taiwan Foreign Trade General Corporation (Taiwan)	July 4, 2003
Tula Instrument Design Bureau (Russia). For alleged sales of laserguided artillery shells to Iran	September 17, 2003 (also designated under Executive Order 12938), removed May 21, 2010
13 entities sanctioned including companies from Russia, China, Belarus, Macedonia, North Korea, UAE, and Taiwan.	April 7, 2004
14 entities from China, North Korea, Belarus, India (two nuclear scientists, Dr. Surendar and Dr. Y.S.R. Prasad), Russia, Spain, and Ukraine.	September 29, 2004
14 entities, mostly from China, for alleged supplying of Iran's missile program. Many, such as North Korea's Changgwang Sinyong and China's Norinco and Great Wall Industry Corp, have been sanctioned several times previously. Newly sanctioned entities included North Korea's Paeksan Associated Corporation, and Taiwan's Ecoma Enterprise Co.	December 2004 and January 2005
9 entities, including those from China (Norinco yet again), India (two chemical companies), and Austria. Sanctions against Dr. Surendar of India (see September 29, 2004) were ended, presumably because of information exonerating him.	December 26, 2005
7 entities. Two Indian chemical companies (Balaji Amines and PrachiPoly Products); two Russian firms (Rosobornexport and aircraft manufacturer Sukhoi); two North Korean entities (Korean Mining and Industrial Development, and Korea Pugang Trading); and one Cuban entity (Center for Genetic Engineering and Biotechnology).	August 4, 2006 (see below for Rosobornexport removal)
9 entities. Rosobornexport, Tula Design, and Komna Design Office of Machine Building, and Alexei Safonov (Russia); Zibo Chemical, China National Aerotechnology, and China National Electrical (China). Korean Mining and Industrial Development (North Korea) for WMD or advanced weapons sales to Iran (and Syria).	January2007 (see below for Tula and Rosoboronexport removal)
14 entities, including Lebanese Hezbollah. Some were penalized for transactions with Syria. Among the new entities sanctioned for assisting Iran were Shanghai Non-Ferrous Metals Pudong Development Trade Company (China); Iran's Defense Industries Organization; Sokkia Company (Singapore); Challenger Corporation (Malaysia); Target Airfreight (Malaysia); Aerospace Logistics Services(Mexico); and Arif Durrani (Pakistani national).	April 23, 2007
13 entities: China Xinshidai Co.; China Shipbuilding and Offshore International Corp.; Huazhong CNC (China); IRGC; Korea Mining Development Corp. (North Korea); Korea Taesong Trading Co. (NK); Yolin/Yullin Tech, Inc. (South Korea); Rosoboronexport (Russia sate arms export agency); Sudan Master Technology; Sudan Technical Center Co; Army Supply Bureau (Syria); R and M International FZCO (UAE); Venezuelan Military Industries Co.(CAVIM);	October 23, 2008. Rosoboronexport removed May 21, 2010.

16 entities: Belarus: Belarusian Optical Mechanical Association; Beltech Export; China: Karl Lee; Dalian Sunny Industries; Dalian Zhongbang Chemical Industries Co.; Xian Junyun Electronic; Iran: Milad Jafari; DIO; IRISL; Qods Force; SAD Import-Export; SBIG; North Korea: Tangun Trading; Syria: Industrial Establishment of Defense; Scientific Studies and Research Center; Venezuela: CAVIM.	May 23, 2011

Entities Designated as Threats to Iraqi Stability under Executive Order 13438

Ahmad Forouzandeh. Commander of the Qods Force Ramazan Headquarters, accused of fomenting sectarian violence in Iraq and of organizing training in Iran for Iraqi Shiite militia fighters	January 9, 2008
Abu Mustafa al-Sheibani. Iran based leader of network that funnels Iranian arms to Shiite militias in Iraq.	January 9, 2008
Isma'il al-Lami (Abu Dura). Shiite militia leader, breakaway from Sadr Mahdi Army, alleged to have committed mass kidnapings and planned assassination attempts against Iraqi Sunni politicians	January 9, 2008
Mishan al-Jabburi. Financier of Sunni insurgents, owner of proinsurgent Al-Zawra television, now banned	January 9, 2008
Al Zawra Television Station	January 9, 2008
Khata'ib Hezbollah (pro-Iranian Mahdi splinter group)	July 2, 2009
Abu Mahdi al-Muhandis	July 2, 2009

Iranians Sanctioned Under September 29, 2010, Executive Order 13553 on Human Rights Abusers

1. IRGC Commander Mohammad Ali Jafari 2. Minister of Interior at time of June 2009 elections Sadeq Mahsouli 3. Minister of Intelligence at time of elections Qolam Hossein Mohseni-Ejei 4. Tehran Prosecutor General at time of elections Saeed Mortazavi 5. Minister of Intelligence Heydar Moslehi 6. Former Defense Minister Mostafa Mohammad Najjar 7. Deputy National Police Chief Ahmad Reza Radan 8. Basij (security militia) Commander at time of elections Hossein Taeb	All sanctioned on September 29, 2010
9. Tehran Prosecutor General Abbas Dowlatabadi (appointed August 2009). Has indicted large numbers of Green movement protesters. 10. Basij forces commander (since October 2009) Mohammad Reza Naqdi (was head of Basij intelligence during post 2009 election crackdown)	Sanctioned on February 23, 2011
11. Islamic Revolutionary Guad Corps (IRGC) 12. Basij Resistance Force 13. Law Enforcement Forces (LEF) 14. LEF Commander Ismail Ahmad Moghadam	June 9, 2011.

Table 6. (Continued)

Iranians Sanctioned Under Executive Order 13572 (April 29, 2011) for Repression of the Syrian People	
- Revolutionary Guard – Qods Force	April 29, 2011
- Qasem Soleimani (Qods Force Commander)	May 18, 2011
- Mohsen Chizari (Commander of Qods Force operations and training)	Same as above

End Notes

[1] As amended by CISADA (P.L. 111-195), these definitions include pipelines to or through Iran, as well as contracts to lead the construction, upgrading, or expansions of energy projects. CISADA also changes the definition of investment to eliminate the exemption from sanctions for sales of energy-related equipment to Iran, if such sales are structured as investments or ongoing profit-earning ventures.

[2] Under Section 4(d) of the original act, for Iran, the threshold dropped to $20 million, from $40 million, one year after enactment, when U.S. allies did not join a multilateral sanctions regime against Iran. However, P.L. 111-195 explicit sets the threshold investment level at $20 million. For Libya, the threshold was $40 million, and sanctionable activity included export to Libya of technology banned by Pan Am 103-related Security Council Resolutions 748 (March 31, 1992) and 883 (November 11, 1993).

[3] The definition of energy sector had included oil and natural gas, but now, as a consequence of the enactment of P.L. 111-195, also includes liquefied natural gas (LNG), oil or LNG tankers, and products to make or transport pipelines that transport oil or LNG.

[4] Taking responsibility for constructing oil refineries or petrochemical plants in Iran did constitute sanctionable projects under the original version of ISA because ISA's definition of investment includes "responsibility for the development of petroleum resources located in Iran." *Table 5* provides some information on openly announced contracts to upgrade or refurbish Iranian oil refineries.

[5] Other ISA amendments under that law included recommending against U.S. nuclear agreements with countries that supply nuclear technology to Iran and expanding provisions of the USA Patriot Act (P.L. 107-56) to curb money-laundering for use to further WMD programs.

[6] This latter termination requirement added by P.L. 109-293. This law also removed Libya from the act, although application to Libya effectively terminated when the president determined on April 23, 2004, that Libya had fulfilled the requirements of all U.N. resolutions on Pan Am 103.

[7] Dollar figures for investments in Iran represent public estimates of the amounts investing firms are expected to spend over the life of a project, which might in some cases be several decades.

[8] Text of announcement of waiver decision by then Secretary of State Madeleine Albright, containing expectation of similar waivers in the future. http://www.parstimes.com/law/albright_southpars.html.

[9] Much of this section is derived from a meeting between the CRS author and officials of the State Department's Economics Bureau, which is tasked with the referenced review of investment projects. November 24, 2009.

[10] Prior to CISADA, the definition of investment in ISA specifically exempted sales of equipment or services under that definition. CISADA omitted that exclusion.

[11] http://www.kuwaittimes.net/read_news.php?newsid=NDQ0OTY1NTU4; http://english. fars news.com/newstext.php? nn=8901181055.

[12] For example, Bijan Kajehpour of Atieh Consulting. Presentation at CSIS, October 4, 2011.

[13] The executive order was issued under the authority of: The International Emergency Economic Powers Act (IEEPA, 50 USC. 1701 et seq.; the National Emergencies Act (50 USC. 1601 et seq.; Section 505 of the International Security and Development Cooperation Act of 1985 (22 USC. 2349aa-9) and Section 301 of Title 3, United States Code. An August 1997 amendment to the trade ban (Executive Order 13059) prevented U.S. companies from knowingly exporting goods to a third country for incorporation into products destined for Iran.

[14] The information in this bullet is taken from: Becker, Jo. "With U.S. Leave, Companies Skirt Iran Sanctions." *New York Times*, December 24, 2010.

[15] Form 10-K Filed for fiscal year ended December 31, 2008.

[16] Prada, Paulo, and Betsy McKay. Trading Outcry Intensifies. *Wall Street Journal*, March 27, 2007; Brush, Michael. Are You Investing in Terrorism? MSN Money, July 9, 2007.

[17] New York Times, March 7, 2010, cited previously.

[18] Subsidiaries of the Registrant at December 31, 2009. http://www.sec.gov/Archives/ edgar/ data/780571/ 000078057110000007/ex_21-1.htm.

[19] "Exhibit to 10-K Filed February 25, 2009." Officials of Fluor claim that their only dealings with Iran involve property in Iran owned by a Fluor subsidiary, which the subsidiary has been unable to dispose of. CRS conversation with Fluor, December 2009.

[20] Form 10-K for Fiscal year ended December 31, 2009.

[21] Form 10-K for Fiscal year ended December 31, 2007.

[22] Form 10-K for Fiscal year ended December 31, 2008, claims firm directed its subsidiaries to cease new business in Iran and Cuba, Syria, and Sudan as of September 2007.

[23] Asjylyn Loder and David Evans. "Koch Brothers Flout Law Getting Richer With Iran Sales." Bloomberg News, October 3, 2011.

[24] "Iran Says Halliburton Won Drilling Contract." *Washington Times*, January 11, 2005.

[25] "Caterpillar Says Tightens 'No-Iran' Business Policy." Reuters, March 1, 2010.

[26] Nixon, Ron. "2 Corporations Say Business With Tehran Will Be Curbed." *New York Times*, March 11, 2010.

[27] Baker, Peter. "U.S. and Foreign Companies Feeling Pressure to Sever Ties With Iran." New York Times, April 24, 2010.

[28] Hearing of the Financial Services and General Government Subcommittee of the House Appropriations Committee, *Federal News Service*, May 21, 2009.

[29] Kessler, Glenn. "U.S. Moves to Isolate Iranian Banks." *Washington Post*, September 9, 2006.

[30] http://www.treasury.gov/press-center/press-releases/Pages/tg1367.aspx

[31] Such laws include the Atomic Energy Act of 1954 and the Energy Policy Act of 2005 (P.L. 109-58).

[32] The provision contains certain exceptions to ensure the safety of astronauts, but it nonetheless threatened to limit U.S. access to the international space station after April 2006, when Russia started charging the United States for transportation on its Soyuz spacecraft. Legislation in the 109th Congress (S. 1713, P.L. 109-112) amended the provision in order to facilitate continued U.S. access and extended INA sanctions provisions to Syria.

[33] For information on the steps taken by individual states, see National Conference of State Legislatures. State Divestment Legislation.

[34] Rhoads, Christopher. "Iran's Web Spying Aided by Western Technology." Wall Street Journal, June 22, 2009.

[35] End, Aurelia. "Siemens Quits Iran Amid Mounting Diplomatic Tensions." Agence France Press, January 27, 2010.

[36] Thomas Erdbink. "Iran's Cyber Police Battle the Lure of the Internet." *Washington Post*, October 30. 2011.

[37] U.S. Department of Treasury, Office of Public Affairs. Treasury Sanctions Iranian Security Forces for Human Rights Abuses, June 9, 2011.

[38] http://www.treasury.gov/resource-center/sanctions/Documents/tar2010.pdf.

[39] See CRS Report RL31258, *Suits Against Terrorist States by Victims of Terrorism*, by Jennifer K. Elsea.

[40] Text of the resolution is at http://www.isis-online.org/uploads/isis-reports/documents/ Draft_ resolution_on_Iran_annexes.pdf.

[41] Letter signed by eleven U.S. Senators to German Foreign Minister Guido Westerwelle. February 1, 2011.

[42] Warrick, Joby. "Iran Using Fronts to Get Bomb Parts From U.S." *Washington Post*, January 11, 2009; Institute for Science and International Security. "Iranian Entities' Illicit Military Procurement Networks." David Albright, Paul Brannan, and Andrea Scheel. January 12, 2009.

[43] During the active period of talks, which began in December 2002, there were working groups focused not only on the TCA terms and proliferation issues but also on Iran's human rights record, Iran's efforts to derail the Middle East peace process, Iranian-sponsored terrorism, counter-narcotics, refugees, migration issues, and the Iranian opposition PMOI.

[44] Speech by National Security Adviser Tom Donilon at the Brookings Institution. November 22, 2011.

[45] The text of the report is at http://www.isis-online.org/uploads/isis-reports/documents/ Iran_24 May2011.pdf.

[46] "Iran's Gateway in Dubai Highlights Sanctions Bite." *Associated Press*, February 1, 2011.

[47] International Monetary Fund. IMF Country Report No. 11/241. August 2011.

[48] Mufson, Steven and Robin Wright. "Iran Adapts to Economic Pressure." *Washington Post,* October 29, 2007.

[49] Speech by Stuart Levey before the Center for Strategic and International Studies. September 20, 2010.

[50] Erdbink, Thomas. "Leaving Iran's Middle Class Behind." *Washington Post,* November 7, 2010.

[51] Khajehpour presentation at CSIS. Op. cit.

[52] GAO. GAO-11-855R. Firms Reported in Open Sources As Having Commercial Activity in Iran's Oil, Gas, and Petrochemical Sectors. August 3, 2011.

[53] http://online.wsj.com/article/SB10001424052748704569204575328851816763476.html.

[54] Stockman, Farah. "Oil Firm Says It Will Withdraw From Iran." Boston Globe, November 12, 2010.

[55] "Iran Revolutionary Guards Pull Out of Gas Deal Over Sanctions." *Platts*, July 19, 2010.

[56] Information in this section derived from, Blas, Javier. "Traders Cut Iran Petrol Line." Financial Times, March 8, 2010.

[57] Information provided at Foundation for Defense of Democracies conference on Iran. December 9, 2010.

[58] Becker, Jo and Ron Nixon. "U.S. Enriches Companies Defying Its Policy on Iran." *New York Times*, March 7, 2010.

[59] GAO-10-967R. Exporters of Refined Petroleum Products to Iran. September 3, 2010.

[60] http://www.ft.com/cms/s/0/009370f0-486e-11df-9a5d-00144feab49a.html.

[61] http://www.defenddemocracy.org/index.php?option=com_content&task=view&id= 1178811 5&Itemid=105.

[62] http://www.defenddemocracy.org/index.php?option=com_ content&task=view&id=117881 15 &Itemid=105.

[63] http://www.defenddemocracy.org/index.php?option =com_content&task=view&id=117881 15 &Itemid=105.

In: The Sanctions Squeeze on Iran and Syria ISBN: 978-1- 62081-015-6
Editors: M. H. Rocha and R. L. Puckett

Chapter 2

UNREST IN SYRIA AND U.S. SANCTIONS AGAINST THE ASAD REGIME*

Jeremy M. Sharp and Christopher M. Blanchard

SUMMARY

This report analyzes the unrest in Syria and the U.S. response to the Syrian government's crackdown against demonstrators. It also provides background information on U.S. sanctions against the Asad regime and its supporters.

A variety of U.S. legislative provisions and executive directives prohibit direct foreign assistance funding to Syria and restrict bilateral trade relations, largely because of the U.S. State Department's designation of Syria as a sponsor of international terrorism. On December 12, 2003, President George W. Bush signed the Syria Accountability Act, P.L. 108-175, which imposed additional economic sanctions against Syria. Syrian individuals and government officials are subject to targeted financial sanctions pursuant to executive orders relating to terrorism, proliferation, and regional security. Successive administrations have designated several Syrian entities as weapons proliferators and sanctioned several Russian companies for alleged weapons of mass destruction or advanced weapons sales to Syria.

---

* This is an edited, reformatted and augmented version of a Congressional Research Service publication, CRS Report for Congress RL33487, prepared for Members and Committees of Congress, from www.crs.gov, dated November 9, 2011.

The following legislation introduced in the 112th Congress addresses the current situation in Syria.

- H.R. 2106, The Syria Freedom Support Act. Sanctions the development of petroleum resources of Syria, the production of refined petroleum products in Syria, and the exportation of refined petroleum products to Syria.
- H.Res. 296 (S.Res. 180 in the Senate). Expresses support for peaceful demonstrations and universal freedoms in Syria and condemns the human rights violations by the Assad Regime.
- H.R. 2105, The Iran, North Korea, and Syria Nonproliferation Reform and Modernization Act of 2011. States that it shall be U.S. policy to fully implement and enforce sanctions against Iran, North Korea, and Syria for their proliferation activities and policies.
- S. 1048, The Iran, North Korea, and Syria Sanctions Consolidation Act of 2011. Amends the Iran, North Korea, and Syria Nonproliferation Act to include in the scope of such act a person that (1) acquired materials mined or extracted within North Korea's territory or control; or (2) provided shipping services for the transportation of goods to or from Iran, North Korea, or Syria relating to such countries' weapons of mass destruction programs, support for acts of international terrorism, or human rights abuses. Excludes from such provisions shipping services for emergency or humanitarian purposes.
- S. 1472, The Syria Sanctions Act of 2011. Denies companies that conduct business in Syria's energy sector (investment, oil purchases, and sale of gasoline) access to U.S. financial institutions and requires federal contractors to certify that they are not engaged in sanctionable activity.

UPRISING AND CRACKDOWN IN SYRIA

For a full account of recent events and an assessment of their implications, see "Current Status."

Overview: Syria's Changing Political Landscape and Repercussions for U.S. Policy

The Asad family has ruled Syria since 1970. President Bashar al Asad, like his father Hafez al Asad before him, has wielded almost total control over domestic politics and has steered the country's outsized foreign policy to play key roles in multiple arenas in the Middle East (Lebanon, Israel-Palestine, Iran, and Iraq) despite Syria's small size and lack of resources. Now, with the country in turmoil, many observers are interested in how prolonged Syrian instability (or a possible changing of the guard there) might affect other U.S. foreign policy priorities in the region, such as Lebanese stability and countering Hezbollah; limiting Iranian influence; and solving the Arab-Israeli conflict. Unlike in Egypt, where the United States has provided support to the military and democracy assistance to newly empowered political groups, the U.S. role in Syria is more limited. Some U.S. sanctions are already in place and Syria has been ineligible for U.S. aid due to its inclusion on the State Sponsor of Terrorism list. Military and intelligence cooperation is sporadic and limited. Thus the role the United States can play in Syria's evolving domestic crisis is in question, and policymakers may be searching for channels of influence in order to preserve U.S. interests in a rapidly changing political landscape.

As of November 8, 2011, the United Nations High Commissioner for Human Rights estimates that that over 3,500 civilians have been killed. In addition, Syrian human rights groups report that over 12,000 Syrian protestors have been arrested.

Current Status

More than 3,500 people have been killed during the uprising in Syria according to official estimates. The actual figure may be much higher. In addition, between 11,000 and 25,000 people have fled the country due to violence or regime threats against protestors and their families. Activists estimate that tens of thousands of people have been detained for organizing or participating in anti-government demonstrations. Despite the Syrian government's recent formal agreement to an Arab League-proposed end to the government crackdown, most observers expect violence between regime forces and protestors to continue for some time.

Unrest in Syria shows no sign of abating, and much uncertainty persists regarding the country's future. Some experts believe that the Alawite-dominated regime, in one form or another (perhaps without Asad family rule), can remain in power. Others believe that a sectarian war is likely and that recent violent clashes between Alawites and Sunnis reflect a trend toward heightened intercommunal conflict. Another view posits that international sanctions are working, and that economic pressure may eventually topple the regime perhaps within the next two years. Finally, some fear that the violence within Syria's borders may spread elsewhere, with what has been a domestic conflict turning regional due to possible Sunni-Shiite tensions, a Syrian or Hezbollah provocation of Israel, or transnational Kurdish restiveness in Syria-Turkey-Iraq-Iran border areas.

Within Syria, protests continue nationwide, though central Damascus and Aleppo, the two largest cities, have remained quieter than most areas. The frequency of protests has remained steady, although unconfirmed reports suggest that in some cities, protest turnouts are diminishing. The opposition has begun to coalesce around a new umbrella organization, the Syrian National Council (SNC), most of whose members are exiles. Inside Syria, some local activists question SNC positions and leadership. The SNC remains officially committed to non-violent, peaceful protest. However new rebel groups composed of defected soldiers espouse and are conducting armed resistance. Most Syrians still reject international military intervention, though some have stated their support for U.N.-mandated assistance.[1]

Various urban and rural areas (Dara'a, Hama, Idlib, Rastan, Deir Al Zour) have experienced regime-opposition clashes, but none more so than Homs, Syria's third largest city. There, local fighters and army defectors reportedly are protecting whole neighborhoods from regime security forces, and casualties on both sides occur daily. Civilians in some areas are confined to their houses. In recent weeks, there has been a spate of reportedly sectarian-motivated killings of doctors, a nuclear engineer, and professors. However, some reports indicate that some Alawites inside Homs are opposed to the government crackdown.[2] In early November, regime forces have attempted to retake areas of Homs controlled by defectors, allegedly deploying tanks to the Baba Amr area of Homs in attempt to wipe out rebel forces based there. According to one opposition figure, "The defectors and the people don't have enough weapons or strength to wage a war against a professional and disciplined army. We cannot talk about a war between them because they're not equal powers. It's impossible for defectors to keep the city."[3]

Fear of all-out sectarian warfare, akin to the situation in Iraq between 2006 and 2008, may drive many religious minorities to continue their support for the Asad regime. Some Christians have participated in and are leaders of the protest movement, yet many are at least still publicly hesitant to withdraw their support from the government. Christian religious leaders have been especially vocal lately in articulating their communities' ongoing support for the Asad regime, as have some Lebanese Christian leaders.[4]

In order to bolster its claim that it is at least attempting to adopt political reforms, the Syrian government has taken formal steps toward liberalization, though many skeptics doubt the regime's intentions to truly promote political pluralism in the midst of a brutal crackdown. In April, the regime abolished the Emergency Law, though it has continued its apparently unlawful detention of protestors. To date, the government has pledged to implement a new political parties law[5] to allow for competition with the ruling Ba'ath party; to implement a new media law to promote press freedom; to implement a new decree to allow for more competition for state jobs; to hold parliamentary elections in early 2012; and to rewrite the constitution. In addition, several pro-regime rallies have taken place in recent months, with crowds estimated by government sources to be as large as 100,000. The Syrian government continues to place the blame for instability on terrorist elements with external support.

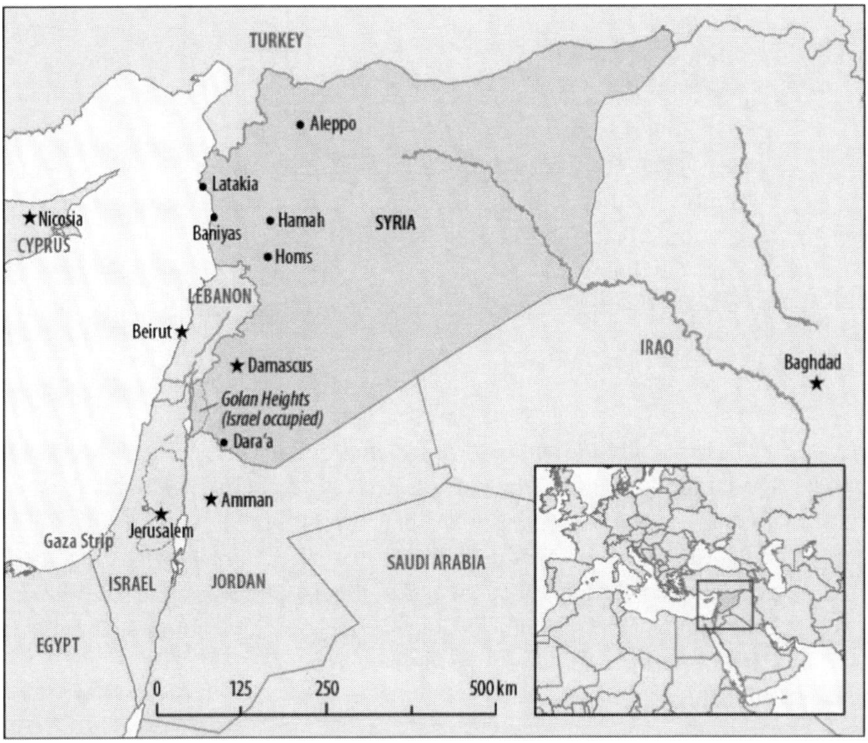

Source: CRS Graphics.

Figure 1. Map of Syria.

The Syrian Opposition and Armed Resistance

Syrian opposition groups have grown increasingly organized as the uprising has unfolded, but remain divided over strategy and tactics. Local Coordinating Councils active in many areas create an informal network linking activists around the country. Two opposition coalition groups, one based in Syria and the other based in neighboring Turkey, are seeking to shape the political agenda and strategy of the movement:

- The *Syrian National Council (SNC)* was formally organized in Turkey in October 2011 and brings together a range of external activists, along with representatives of the Damascus Declaration Forces for National and Democratic Change, the Syrian Muslim Brotherhood, and the Syrian Revolution General Commission (SRGC). The National Council has called for "immediate protection for civilians," in contrast to some of its domestic counterparts. The Council alsofirmly believes that dialogue with the Asad government is impossible. The Council rejected the Arab League agreement with the Syrian government on November 2 (see below), and called on the Arab League "to freeze Syria's membership, ensure the protection of civilians and recognize the SNC as the representative of the Syrian revolution." Prominent leaders of the SNC include Council chairman Burhan Ghalyun, a France-based Syrian academic, and Muhammad Riyad al Shaqfah, the Controller General of the Syrian Muslim Brotherhood.
- The *National Coordination Commission of the Forces of Democratic Change (NCC)* is a Syria-based alliance of leftist groups, Kurdish activists, and individuals associated with the 2005 Damascus Declaration on political reform. The NCC has criticized calls for any civilian protection measures that might invite external military intervention and has left open the prospect of dialogue with the Syrian government, predicated on an end to the use of force against civilians. Prominent leaders of the NCC include general coordinator Hassan Abd al Azim and long-time domestic opposition activists such as Michel Kilo.

Reports from Syria increasingly suggest that dissident military personnel and officers, many acting under the aegis of two organizations called the Free Syrian Army and the Free Officers Movement, are actively targeting government security forces in armed attacks. Free Syrian Army forces are rumored to number several hundred personnel, but precise and verifiable estimates are not available.

Public accounts further suggest that thousands of Syrian military and security personnel may have defected during the uprising as forces have been increasingly stretched geographically and logistically and as individuals have rejected orders to crack down on civilian protestors. The Syrian government has condemned the use of force against state security personnel and attributes the growing number of attacks on military and police forces to "terrorists" and armed Islamists.

The use of force by Syrian opposition groups raises fundamental questions about the nature and future of the Syrian uprising. It also is complicating internal opposition debates over strategy and tactics. Some groups view force as a necessary and appropriate response to the violently repressive tactics being used by government personnel. Others argue that the use of force opens the opposition to criticism, undercuts its international legitimacy, and could increase fear among "fence sitting" supporters of the government about the likelihood of violent chaos in the wake of regime change. The debate over the use of force is an extension of the broader political debate that divides the leading opposition groups over the possibility of dialogue with the Asad government. Those who view the government as disingenuous in its offers of reform and dialogue may be more likely to support or acquiesce to the use of force as the political confrontation continues.

International Reactions and Policy Responses

Syria's geographic location, its diverse population, and its leaders' foreign policy tactics raise the stakes of the current political confrontation for Syria's neighbors and the international community. Destabilizing refugee flows, cross-border sectarian rivalries, the future of regional terrorist groups, the prospect of weapons proliferation, and potential changes to regional power dynamics all hang in the balance.

Syria's Neighbors

To date, Syria's neighbors have taken cautious and concerned approaches in response to the country's unrest. Groups in each country have particular concerns about conflict in Syria potentially having destabilizing effects on their national security and diverse populations. Turkey has been the most vocal and involved of Syria's neighbors to date, and the government of Turkish Prime Minister Recep Tayyip Erdoğan has shifted its approach from seeking to foster dialogue between the Asad government and its critics to hosting Syrian opposition groups and warning of unspecified sanctions or military actions if Syrian authorities continue to use force against civilians.

This change in approach by Turkish Prime Minister Recep Tayyip Erdoğan seems to coincide with his desire to project a regionally populist stance that is not viewed by Arab populations as siding with autocrats or entrenched commercial interests. One of Turkey's concerns is that region-wide unrest, especially in neighboring Syria, could endanger the political stability of the entire area and possibly jeopardize Turkey's political and economic influence in the region.

Lebanese concerns are focused on the potential for conflict or regime change in Syria to affect Lebanon's fragile sectarian balance. Some prominent Lebanese Christians have warned that the rise of Syria's majority Sunni population to power could pose risks to Christians and other religious minorities in Syria and Lebanon. Reciprocally, Syrian officials accuse Lebanese Sunnis of providing shelter and support to armed opposition forces inside Syria. A number of disputed cross-border incidents illustrate rising Lebanese-Syrian tensions. The outsized role that Syria plays in Lebanon's affairs and its role as a lifeline for Hezbollah further raises the stakes of the unrest both for Lebanon and for Israel. Hezbollah has stated its support for the Asad government and both have warned that third-party intervention in Syria's crisis could lead to regional conflagration, widely interpreted as a threat to Israel.

Syria's other neighbors also have their concerns over instability there. In Iraq, Shiites including Prime Minister Nouri al Maliki, may be concerned over the possibility of Syrian Sunni Muslims toppling the Asad regime, and therefore the Prime Minister has supported Asad's promises for reform. In Jordan, the monarchy may be concerned that violence in Syria may lead many Syrians to take refuge in Jordan, though to date fewer than a thousand Syrians are said to have sought refuge in the kingdom. Of all of the neighbors, Syrian unrest places Israel in the most precarious position.

The Syrian regime has been a stable and predictable Israeli adversary for decades. If the Syrian regime fears its downfall may be imminent, Israelis fear that the Asad government could try to instigate a conflict with Israel in order to distract opposition to its rule. Should the Syrian regime fall, Israelis are concerned over its replacement with a more radical Sunni-Islamist government.

Regional and Global Actors

The Asad government has positioned Syria as a pivot point in a number of regional rivalries, complicating efforts by other Middle Eastern governments to take a unified and decisive approach to the current crisis. Syria's role as a facilitator of Iranian support to Hezbollah while serving as host to Hamas and other Sunni terrorist groups is perhaps the most important example of this dynamic. Saudi Arabia's King Abdullah has vigorously criticized the Asad government's use of force against civilians, but many observers believe this may stem more from an interest in countering Iranian regional influence than from genuine concern for the well-being of Syrian nationals. Arab League diplomacy has focused on setting terms for a ceasefire and a resumption of dialogue between the opposition and the government, and the conditions of the agreement announced on November 2 reflect this approach, but they have been met by criticism from Syrian opposition forces and a continuing use of force by Syrian security personnel and some armed opposition groups.

Action at the U.N. Security Council reflects shared concerns among the permanent members of the Security Council about the crisis and its potential spillover effects, along with deep divisions about the way forward. Russia and China jointly vetoed a proposed Security Council resolution in early October, citing concern that a resolution could pave the way for one-sided intervention in the Syrian unrest, and warning of the risks of repeating a scenario like the NATO-led intervention in Libya in the more fragile and geopolitically important environment of the Levant. Critics of the veto point to Russian and Chinese interests in preserving their long-standing arms sales relationships with Syria, protecting the principle of non-intervention, and gaining access to potential energy resources. On November 1, NATO Secretary-General Anders Fogh Rasmussen categorically ruled out the possibility of a NATO-led military intervention in Syria. The European Union has prohibited the purchase of Syrian oil exports, dealing a potentially crippling blow to Syrian state export revenues unless alternatives are found (see below).

U.S. Policy and Sanctions

President Obama and his administration have been calling for Asad's resignation since August. On November 2, after reports surfaced that Syria had agreed to an Arab League-proposed plan to end its crackdown, a State Department spokesperson reiterated the administration position, stating that "Syria's made a lot of promises to the international community in the past. Our position remains that President Assad has lost his legitimacy to rule and should step down."[6] When asked whether or not the United States would intervene militarily in Syria to protect demonstrators, a State Department spokesperson responded that

> "The vast majority of the Syrian opposition continues to speak in favor of peaceful, nonviolent protests and against foreign intervention of any kind, and particularly foreign military intervention into the situation in Syria, and we respect that."[7] Some U.S. officials have publicly indicated their belief that President Asad will not be able to remain in office over time. According to Secretary of Defense Leon Panetta, "While he continues to resist, I think it's very clear that it's a matter of time before that (exit) in fact happens. When it does, we don't know."[8]

In response to unspecified threats against the recently confirmed U.S. Ambassador to Syria, Robert S. Ford, the ambassador returned to Washington, D.C. in October. Ford had been previously targeted by pro-government demonstrators who obstructed a meeting he conducted with opposition activists in September 2011.

The administration has continued to expand U.S. sanctions on Syria while advocating further multilateral sanctions. Table 1 (below) summarizes U.S. sanctions activity since the start of the Syria uprising in March 2011.

Congressional Action

The Syrian government's use of lethal force in response to political demonstrations has refocused attention on the basic tenets of U.S. policy toward Syria. Some members of Congress and nongovernmental observers argue that the recent violence demonstrates the futility of expecting any substantive reform by Syrian authorities and suggests that U.S. policy should shift toward outright confrontation and embrace regime change as a policy goal.

While the administration has called for President Asad to step down, arguments in favor of regime change have been accompanied by wariness about what the implications of confrontation would be, and what the implications of regime change would be for regional security, particularly in light of the delicate sectarian balance in the Levant and a lack of established U.S. relationships with government and non-government actors in Syria.

Table A-1. U.S.-Syrian Trade Statistics 2005-2010 ($ in millions)

	2005	2006	2007	2008	2009	2010
U.S. Exports to Syria	$155.0	$224.3	$361.4	$408.8	$300.0	$506.2
U.S. Imports from Syria	$323.5	$213.7	$110.5	$352.0	$285.9	$428.7
Totals	$478.5	$438.0	$471.9	$760.8	$585.9	$934.9

Source: TradeStats Express – National Trade Data, Presented by the Office of Trade and Industry Information (OTII), Manufacturing and Services, International Trade Administration, U.S. Department of Commerce.

Table 1. U.S. Sanctions Against Syria in 2011 (Implemented by Treasury Department's Office of Foreign Assets Control [OFAC])

Date	Sanctioned Individual/Entity	Sanction or Related Activity Description
October 3, 2011, Treasury Department		OFAC issued two general licenses related to Syria to authorize payments in connection with overflight or emergency landing and transactions with respect to telecommunications
September 27, 2011, Treasury Department		OFAC issued a General Licenses related to Syria to authorize third-country diplomatic and consular funds transfers and to authorize certain services in support of nongovernmental organizations' activities.
September 9, 2011, Treasury Department		OFAC issued four general licenses related to Syria to authorize wind down transactions, certain official activities of international organizations, incidental transactions related to U.S. persons residing in Syria and operation of accounts.

Table 1. (Continued)

Date	Sanctioned Individual/Entity	Sanction or Related Activity Description
August 30, 2011, Treasury Department	Walid Mouallem (Foreign Minister), Ali Abdul Karim Ali (Syrian Ambassador to Lebanon), Bouthaina Shaaban (Advisor to the President)	Added to OFAC's Specially Designated Nationals (SDN) List
August 18, 2011, Executive Order 13582	Government of Syria	Freezes all assets of the Government of Syria, prohibits U.S. persons from engaging in any transaction involving the Government of Syria, bans U.S. imports of Syrian-origin petroleum or petroleum products, prohibits U.S. persons from having any dealings in or related to Syria's petroleum or petroleum products, and prohibits U.S. persons from operating or investing in Syria.
August 18, 2011, Treasury Department	General Petroleum Corporation, Syrian Company For Oil Transport, Syrian Gas Company, Syrian Petroleum Company, Sytrol	Added to OFAC's SDN List
August 10, 2011, Treasury Department	Commercial Bank of Syria and its Lebanon-based subsidiary, Syrian Lebanese Commercial Bank, Syriatel, the country's main mobile phone operator	Added to OFAC's SDN List
August 4, 2011, Treasury Department	Muhammad Hamsho (businessman with ties to Asad family), Hamsho International Group	Added to OFAC's SDN List
June 29, 2011, Treasury Department	Jamil Hassan (Head of Air Force Intelligence), Political Security Directorate (PSD, domestic intelligence)	Added to OFAC's SDN List

Date	Sanctioned Individual/Entity	Sanction or Related Activity Description
May 18, 2011, Executive Order 13573	President Bashar al Asad, Farouk al Shara (vice president), Adel Safar (prime minister), Mohammad Ibrahim al Shaar (minister of the interior), Ali Habib Mahmoud (minister of defense), Abdul Fatah Qudsiya (head of Syrian military intelligence), Mohammed Dib Zaitoun (director of political security directorate), Nabil Rafik al Kuzbari, General Mohsen Chizari (Commander of Iran Revolutionary Guard Corp Qods Force suspected of human rights abuses in Syria), Al Mashreq Investment Fund, Bena Properties, Cham Holding, Syrian Air Force Intelligence, Syrian Military Intelligence, Syrian National Security Bureau	Added to OFAC's SDN List
April 29, 2011, Executive Order 13572	Maher al Asad, Ali Mamluk (director of the Syrian General Intelligence Directorate GID), Atif Najib (former head of the Syrian Political Security Directorate for Dara'a province and the president's cousin). the General Intelligence Directorate, and Iran's Islamic Revolutionary Guard Corps – Quds Force (for allegedly assisting Syria in its crackdown)	Added to OFAC's SDN List

Source: U.S. Treasury Department.

Notes: As part of its enforcement efforts, OFAC publishes a list of individuals and companies owned or controlled by, or acting for or on behalf of, targeted countries. It also lists individuals, groups, and entities, such as terrorists and narcotics traffickers designated under programs that are not country-specific. Collectively, such individuals and companies are called Specially Designated Nationals or SDNs. Their assets are blocked and U.S. persons are generally prohibited from dealing with them.

Other lawmakers have urged a gradual approach of increasing multilateral political condemnation and economic pressure against the Asad regime.

The following legislation introduced in the 112th Congress addresses the current situation in Syria.

- H.R. 2106, The Syria Freedom Support Act—Would, among other things, sanction the development of petroleum resources of Syria, the production of refined petroleum products in Syria, and the exportation of refined petroleum products to Syria.
- H.Res. 296 (S.Res. 180 in the Senate), A Resolution Expressing support for peaceful demonstrations and universal freedoms in Syria and condemning the human rights violations by the Assad Regime—Among other things, it urges the "president to continue to work with the European Union, the government of Turkey, the Arab League, the Gulf Cooperation Council, and other allies and partners to bring an end to human rights abuses in Syria, hold the perpetrators accountable, and support the aspirations of the people of Syria."
- H.R. 2105, The Iran, North Korea, and Syria Nonproliferation Reform and Modernization Act of 2011—States that it shall be U.S. policy to fully implement and enforce sanctions against Iran, North Korea, and Syria for their proliferation activities and policies. Would, among other things, prohibit U.S. nuclear cooperation agreements and related export licenses and transfers of materials, services and goods with a country that is assisting the nuclear program of Iran, North Korea, or Syria, or is transferring advanced conventional weapons to such countries.
- S. 1048, The Iran, North Korea, and Syria Sanctions Consolidation Act of 2011— Amends the Iran, North Korea, and Syria Nonproliferation Act to include in the scope of such act a person that (1) acquired materials mined or extracted within North Korea's territory or control; or (2) provided shipping services for the transportation of goods to or from Iran, North Korea, or Syria relating to such countries' weapons of mass destruction programs, support for acts of international terrorism, or human rights abuses. Excludes from such provisions shipping services for emergency or humanitarian purposes.
- S. 1472, The Syria Sanctions Act of 2011—Denies companies that conduct business in Syria's energy sector (investment, oil purchases, and sale of gasoline) access to U.S. financial institutions and requires

federal contractors to certify that they are not engaged in sanctionable activity.

Syria's Economy under Strain

Though more robust Western sanctions on Syria have only recently been enacted, early reports indicate that the Syrian economy and national budget are suffering due to a drop in oil exports resulting from sanctions, months of domestic unrest and the loss of international tourism

revenues, and new social and military spending aimed at quelling public anger. In September, the International Monetary Fund indicated that it expects Syria's economy to contract by 2% this year.

The Syrian government has responded somewhat erratically to its negative economic outlook. In order to preserve hard currency, the government initially banned almost all imported goods, leading to price hikes, inflation, and shortages of many basic items. After 12 days, it rescinded the ban, concerned about angering the private sector in Damascus and Aleppo, which has largely been supportive of the regime. The Central Bank of Syria says that it has $18 billion in foreign exchange reserves and can cover import costs for up to a year. In addition, in late September the Syrian government surprised many when it announced a massive increase in domestic spending, precisely at the same time as new international sanctions were taking effect. The government approved a 58% increase in the state budget, bringing it to $26.5 billion according to official estimates. Food and energy subsidies account for 30% of the total budget.

Sanctions and Syria's Oil and Gas Sector

With the loss of European markets due to an oil export ban, Western countries have denied Syria a major source of revenue and hard currency (25%-30% of total government revenue or $4 billion a year). Before sanctions, the main buyers of approximately 150,000 barrels per day (bpd) of exported Syrian oil were Italy, Germany, France, the Netherlands, Austria, Spain and Turkey. Syria produces about 380,000 bpd total. Existing foreign producers inside Syria are still able to maintain operations, though many foreign companies, including Gulfsands Petroleum (UK), Royal Dutch Shell, Total (France), CNPC (China), and ONGC (India), have cut back production because alternative buyers have yet to surface and Syria has limited domestic refining and storage capacity. Western countries also have banned new investment in Syria's oil and gas sector. These include Canada, which announced a new investment ban in October. The Calgary-based Suncor Energy Inc. already is an existing partner with Syria's General Petroleum Corp in a $1.2 billion Ebla natural gas project. In mid October, another Canadian company, Mena Hydrocarbons Inc, said that it had suspended drilling in Syria due to political turmoil in the country. Sanctions also are having an impact on other aspects of Syria's energy sector, including financing and shipping. According to one oil products trader based in the Middle East, "I don't do Syria anymore. Sanctions appeared tougher, so I gave up.... The problem is getting a bank to finance it and a ship owner to go there."[9]

Since new sanctions were enacted, many analysts have speculated about whether new investors and foreign markets would arise for Syrian oil exports, albeit at lower prices due to sanctions and increased shipping costs. Some experts believe that both India and China are in a position to refine the heavy crude that Syria exports, and some reports suggest that India's ONGC is considering importing oil it currently produces in Syria to India, instead of shutting down its field operations.[10] According to one energy expert, "There is almost certainly someone who will buy it.... In the past there have been trading companies that would launder oil for Iraq or Iran, for example. Some countries will buy gasoline from Caribbean refiners without knowing the origin of the oil."[11] However, others assert that some Asian buyers would find the prospect of purchasing Syrian oil too risky. According to one report, "As far as Chinese and the Indians are concerned, they could of course try to buy some volumes. But the economics don't make any sense for them and volumes are too small to take the risks."[12]

Options and Uncertainty

At present, all eyes are fixed on the Syrian government and opposition's possible responses to the Arab League ceasefire and dialogue proposal. Fighting in and around the city of Homs appears to signal the Asad government's determination to quell resistance with force, and many in the region and internationally are interpreting the siege of Homs as a rejection of the Arab League agreement. Should the government follow through on its commitments to withdraw military forces from cities and reengage in dialogue with opposition, prolonged violence and potential sectarian escalation may be avoided. If opposition forces halt attacks on government personnel and are able to engage in dialogue with the government in a unified fashion, then prospects for a smoother transition to more open political competition could improve.

It appears unlikely that international diplomacy focused on a new round of Security Council-backed sanctions or the possible referral of the situation in Syria to the International Criminal Court (ICC) will resume in earnest until the response of both sides to the Arab League initiative becomes clearer. Russia and China appear adamant that further sanctions targeting the Syrian government are unwarranted and argue that the international community should not overlook the use of force by Syrian opposition groups. The Security Council's response to the Libyan conflict revived a broad international debate over the effect of referrals to the ICC on the decisions of indicted leaders and officials facing calls for their resignation. Intransigence by the Asad government and disunity among Syrian opposition forces could alter regional and global policy calculations on these issues.

President Asad has taken a number of opportunities recently to warn of a regional "earthquake" and prolonged, destabilizing chaos in the event of intervention or the fall of his government. While these warnings have an obvious self-serving purpose, they mirror concerns being expressed by many observers and officials in the region who fear that the types of complications now on display in Libya could have far more dire consequences if they emerge in the more volatile context of the eastern Mediterranean.

Appendix. Previous U.S. Sanctions and Legislation

The following section provides background on U.S. sanctions against Syria. It predates the nation-wide unrest that began in March 2011. For recent information on U.S. sanctions, please see, *Table 1* above.

Overview

Syria remains a U.S.-designated State Sponsor of Terrorism and is therefore subject to a number of U.S. sanctions. Syria was placed on the State Department's State Sponsors of Terrorism List in 1979. Moreover, between 2003 and 2006 Congress passed legislation and President Bush issued new executive orders that expanded U.S. sanctions on Syria. At present, a variety of legislative provisions and executive directives prohibit U.S. aid to Syria and restrict bilateral trade.[13] Principal examples follow.

General Sanctions Applicable to Syria

The International Security Assistance and Arms Export Control Act of 1976 [P.L. 94-329]. Section 303 of this act [90 Stat. 753-754] required termination of foreign assistance to countries that aid or abet international terrorism. This provision was incorporated into the Foreign Assistance Act of 1961 as Section 620A [22 USC 2371]. (Syria was not affected by this ban until 1979, as explained below.)

The International Emergency Economic Powers Act of 1977 [Title II of P.L. 95-223 (codified at 50 USC. §1701 et seq.)]. Under the International Emergency Economic Powers Act (IEEPA), the president has broad powers pursuant to a declaration of a national emergency with respect to a threat "which has its source in whole or substantial part outside the United States, to the national security, foreign policy, or economy of the United States." These powers include the ability to seize foreign assets under U.S. jurisdiction, to prohibit any transactions in foreign exchange, to prohibit payments between financial institutions involving foreign currency, and to prohibit the import or export of foreign currency.

The Export Administration Act of 1979 [P.L. 96-72]. Section 6(i) of this act [93 Stat. 515] required the Secretary of Commerce and the Secretary of State to notify Congress before licensing export of goods or technology valued at more than $7 million to countries determined to have supported acts of international terrorism. (Amendments adopted in 1985 and 1986 relettered Section 6(i) as 6(j) and lowered the threshold for notification from $7 million to $1 million.)

A by-product of these two laws was the so-called state sponsors of terrorism list. This list is prepared annually by the State Department in accordance with Section 6(j) of the Export Administration Act. The list identifies those countries that repeatedly have provided support for acts of international terrorism. Syria has appeared on this list ever since it was first prepared in 1979; it appears most recently in the State Department's annual publication *Country Reports on Terrorism, 2009*, issued on August 5, 2010. Syria's inclusion on this list in 1979 triggered the above-mentioned aid sanctions under P.L. 94-329 and trade restrictions under P.L. 96-72.

Omnibus Diplomatic Security and Antiterrorism Act of 1986 [P.L. 99-399]. Section 509(a) of this act [100 Stat. 853] amended Section 40 of the Arms Export Control Act to prohibit export of items on the munitions list to countries determined to be supportive of international terrorism, thus banning any U.S. military equipment sales to Syria. (This ban was reaffirmed by the

Anti-Terrorism and Arms Export Amendments Act of 1989—see below.) Also, 10 USC. 2249a bans obligation of U.S. Defense Department funds for assistance to countries on the terrorism list.

Omnibus Budget Reconciliation Act of 1986 [P.L. 99-509]. Section 8041(a) of this act [100 Stat. 1962] amended the Internal Revenue Code of 1954 to deny foreign tax credits on income or war profits from countries identified by the Secretary of State as supporting international terrorism. [26 USC 901(j)]. The president was given authority to waive this provision under Section 601 of the Trade and Development Act of 2000 (P.L. 106-200, May 18, 2000).

The Anti-Terrorism and Arms Export Control Amendments Act of 1989 [P.L. 101-222]. Section 4 amended Section 6(j) of the Export Administration Act to impose a congressional notification and licensing requirement for export of goods or technology, irrespective of dollar value, to countries on the terrorism list, if such exports could contribute to their military capability or enhance their ability to support terrorism.

Section 4 also prescribes conditions for removing a country from the terrorism list: prior notification by the president to the Speaker of the House of Representatives and the chairmen of two specified committees of the Senate. In conjunction with the requisite notification, the president must certify that the country has met several conditions that clearly indicate it is no longer involved in supporting terrorist activity. (In some cases, certification must be provided 45 days in advance of removal of a country from the terrorist list).

The Anti-Economic Discrimination Act of 1994 [Part C, P.L. 103-236, the Foreign Relations Authorization Act, FY1994-1995]. Section 564(a) bans the sale or lease of U.S. defense articles and services to any country that questions U.S. firms about their compliance with the Arab boycott of Israel. Section 564(b) contains provisions for a presidential waiver, but no such waiver has been exercised in Syria's case. Again, this provision is moot in Syria's case because of other prohibitions already in effect.

The Antiterrorism and Effective Death Penalty Act of 1996 [P.L. 104-132]. This act requires the president to withhold aid to third countries that provide assistance (Section 325) or lethal military equipment (Section 326) to countries on the terrorism list, but allows the president to waive this provision on grounds of national interest. A similar provision banning aid to third countries that sell lethal equipment to countries on the terrorism list is contained in Section 549 of the Foreign Operations Appropriations Act for FY2001 (H.R. 5526, passed by reference in H.R. 4811, which was signed by President Clinton as P.L. 106-429 on November 6, 2000).

Also, Section 321 of P.L. 104-132 makes it a criminal offense for U.S. persons (citizens or resident aliens) to engage in financial transactions with governments of countries on the terrorism list, except as provided in regulations issued by the Department of the Treasury in consultation with the Secretary of State. In the case of Syria, the implementing regulation prohibits such transactions "with respect to which the United States person knows or has reasonable cause to believe that the financial transaction poses a risk of furthering terrorist acts in the United States." (31 CFR 596, published in the *Federal Register* August 23, 1996, p. 43462.) In the fall of 1996, the then chairman of the House International Relations Committee reportedly protested to then President Clinton about the Treasury Department's implementing regulation, which he described as a "special loophole" for Syria.

In addition to the general sanctions listed above, specific provisions in foreign assistance appropriations legislation enacted since 1981 have barred Syria by name from receiving U.S. aid. The most recent ban appears in Section 7007 of P.L. 111-117, the Consolidated Appropriations Act, 2010, which states that "None of the funds appropriated or otherwise made available pursuant to Titles III through VI of this Act shall be obligated or expended to finance directly any assistance or reparations for the governments of Cuba, North Korea, Iran, or Syria: Provided, That for purposes of this section, the prohibition on obligations or expenditures shall include direct loans, credits, insurance and guarantees of the Export-Import Bank or its agents."

Section 307 of the Foreign Assistance Act of 1961, amended by Section 431 of the Foreign Relations Authorization Act for FY1994-1995 (P.L. 103-236, April 30, 1994), requires the United States to withhold a proportionate share of contributions to international organizations for programs that benefit eight specified countries or entities, including Syria.

The Iran Nonproliferation Act of 2000, P.L. 106-178, was amended by P.L. 109-112 to make its provisions applicable to Syria as well as Iran. The amended act, known as the Iran and Syria Nonproliferation Act, requires the president to submit semi-annual reports to designated congressional committees, identifying any persons involved in arms transfers *to or from* Iran or Syria; also, the act authorizes the president to impose various sanctions against such individuals. On October 13, 2006, President Bush signed P.L. 109-353 which expanded the scope of the original law by adding North Korea to its provisions, thereby renaming the law the Iran, North Korea, and Syria Nonproliferation Act (or INKSNA for short). The list of Syrian entities designated under INKSNA includes Army Supply Bureau (2008), Syrian Navy (2009), Syrian Air Force (2009), and Ministry of Defense (2008).[14] On May

24, 2011, the State Department designated the Industrial Establishment of Defense and Scientific Studies and Research Center (SSRC) under INKSNA.

Specific Sanctions against Syria

Specific U.S. sanctions levied against Syria fall into three main categories: (1) sanctions resulting from the passage of the 2003 Syria Accountability and Lebanese Sovereignty Act (SALSA) that, among other things, prohibit most U.S. exports to Syria; (2) sanctions imposed by executive order from the president that specifically deny certain Syrian citizens and entities access to the U.S. financial system due to their participation in proliferation of weapons of mass destruction, association with Al Qaeda, the Taliban, or Osama bin Laden; or destabilizing activities in Iraq and Lebanon; and (3) sanctions resulting from the USA Patriot Act levied specifically against the Commercial Bank of Syria in 2006.

The 2003 Syria Accountability Act

On December 12, 2003, President Bush signed H.R. 1828, the Syria Accountability and Lebanese Sovereignty Restoration Act into law, as P.L. 108-175. This law requires the president to impose penalties on Syria unless it ceases support for international terrorist groups, ends its occupation of Lebanon, ceases the development of weapons of mass destruction (WMD), and has ceased supporting or facilitating terrorist activity in Iraq (Section 5(a) and 5(d)). Sanctions include bans on the export of military items (already banned under other legislation, see above[15]) and of dual use items (items with both civil and military applications) to Syria (Section 5(a)(1)). In addition, the president is required to impose two or more sanctions from a menu of six:

- a ban on all exports to Syria except food and medicine;
- a ban on U.S. businesses operating or investing in Syria;
- a ban on landing in or overflight of the United States by Syrian aircraft;
- reduction of diplomatic contacts with Syria;
- restrictions on travel by Syrian diplomats in the United States; and
- blocking of transactions in Syrian property (Section 5(a)(2)).

Implementation

On May 11, 2004, President Bush issued Executive Order 13338, implementing the provisions of P.L. 108-175, including the bans on munitions and dual use items (Section 5(a)(1)) and two sanctions from the menu of six listed in Section 5(a)(2). The two sanctions he chose were the ban on exports to Syria other than food and medicine (Section 5(a)(2)(A) and the ban on Syrian aircraft landing in or overflying the United States (Section 5(a)(2)(D). In issuing his executive order, the president stated that Syria has failed to take significant, concrete steps to address the concerns that led to the enactment of the Syria Accountability Act. The president also imposed two additional sanctions based on other legislation.

- Under Section 311 of the USA PATRIOT Act, he instructed the Treasury Department to prepare a rule requiring U.S. financial institutions to sever correspondent accounts with the Commercial Bank of Syria because of money laundering concerns.
- Under the International Emergency Economic Powers Act (IEEPA), he issued instructions to freeze assets of certain Syrian individuals and government entities involved in supporting policies inimical to the United States.

Waivers

In the executive order and in an accompanying letter to Congress, President Bush cited the waiver authority contained in Section 5(b) of the Syria Accountability Act and stated that he wished to issue the following waivers on grounds of national security:

> Regarding Section 5(a)(1) and 5(a)(2)(A): The following exports are permitted: products in support of activities of the U.S. government; medicines otherwise banned because of potential dual use; aircraft parts necessary for flight safety; informational materials; telecommunications equipment to promote free flow of information; certain software and technology; products in support of U.N. operations; and certain exports of a temporary nature.[16]
>
> Regarding Section 5(a)(2)(D): The following operations are permitted: takeoff/landing of Syrian aircraft chartered to transport Syrian officials on official business to the United States; takeoff/landing for non-traffic and non-scheduled stops; takeoff/landing associated with an emergency; and overflights of U.S. territory.

Targeted Financial Sanctions

Since the initial implementation of the Syria Accountability Act (in Executive Order 13338 dated May 2004), the president has repeatedly taken action to sanction individual members of the Asad regime's inner circle.[17] E.O. 13338 declared a national emergency with respect to Syria and authorized the Secretary of the Treasury to block the property of individual Syrians. Based on Section 202(d) of the National Emergencies Act (50 USC. 1622(d)), the president has annually extended his authority to block the property of individual Syrians (latest on April 29, 2011).

When issuing each extension, the president has noted that the actions and policies of the government of Syria continued to pose an unusual and extraordinary threat.[18]

The following individuals and entities have been targeted by the U.S. Treasury Department (Office of Foreign Assets Control or OFAC):

- On June 30, 2005, the U.S. Treasury Department designated two senior Syrian officials involved in Lebanon affairs, Syria's then-Interior Minister and its head of military intelligence in Lebanon (respectively, the late General Kanaan and General Ghazali), as Specially Designated Nationals, thereby freezing any assets they may have in the United States and banning any U.S. persons, including U.S. financial institutions outside of the United States, from conducting transactions with them.[19] Kanaan allegedly committed suicide in October 2005, though some have speculated that he may have been murdered.
- On January 18, 2006, U.S. Treasury Department took the same actions against the president's brother-in-law, Assef Shawkat, chief of military intelligence.
- On April 26, 2006, President Bush issued Executive Order 13399 that authorized the secretary of the Treasury to freeze the U.S.-based assets of anyone found to be involved in the February 2005 assassination of former Lebanese Prime Minister Rafiq Hariri. It also affects anyone involved in bombings or assassinations in Lebanon since October 2004, or anyone hindering the international investigation into the Hariri assassination. The order allows the United States to comply with UNSCR 1636, which calls on all states to freeze the assets of those persons designated by the investigating commission or the government of Lebanon to be involved in the Hariri assassination.

- On August 15, 2006, the U.S. Treasury Department froze assets of two other senior Syrian officers: Major General Hisham Ikhtiyar, for allegedly contributing to Syria's support of foreign terrorist organizations including Hezbollah; and Brigadier General Jama'a Jama'a, for allegedly playing a central part in Syria's intelligence operations in Lebanon during the Syrian occupation.[20]
- On January 4, 2007, the U.S. Treasury Department designated three Syrian entities, the Syrian Higher Institute of Applied Science and Technology, the Electronics Institute, and the National Standards and Calibration Laboratory, as weapons proliferators under an executive order (E.O.13382) based on the authority vested to the president under IEEPA. The three state-sponsored institutions are divisions of Syria's Scientific Studies and Research Center, which was designated by President Bush as a weapons proliferator in June 2005 for research on the development of biological and chemical weapons.[21]
- On August 1, 2007, the president issued E.O. 13441[22] blocking the property of persons undermining the sovereignty of Lebanon or its democratic processes and institutions. On November 5, 2007, the U.S. Treasury Department designated four individuals reportedly affiliated with the Syrian regime's efforts to reassert Syrian control over the Lebanese political system, including Assaad Halim Hardan, Wi'am Wahhab and Hafiz Makhluf (under the authority of E.O.13441) and Muhammad Nasif Khayrbik (under the authority of E.O.13338).[23]
- On February 13, 2008, President Bush issued another Order (E.O.13460) blocking the property of senior Syrian officials. According to the U.S. Treasury Department, the order "targets individuals and entities determined to be responsible for or who have benefitted from the public corruption of senior officials of the Syrian regime. The order also revises a provision in Executive Order 13338 to block the property of Syrian officials who have undermined U.S. and international efforts to stabilize Iraq.[24] One week later, under the authority of E.O.13460, the U.S. Treasury Department froze the U.S. assets and restricted the financial transactions of Rami Makhluf, the 38-year-old cousin of President Bashar al Asad. Makhluf is a powerful Syrian businessman who serves as an interlocutor between foreign investors and Syrian companies. According to one report, "Since a military coup in 1969, the Asads have controlled politics while the Makhlufs have been big business players. The tradition continues in the next generation, with Bashar al-Assad (sic) as

president and Rami Makhluf as a leading force in business."[25] Makhluf is a major stakeholder in Syriatel, the country's largest mobile phone operator. In 2008, the Turkish company Turkcell was in talks to purchase Syriatel, but, according to *Reuters*, negotiations over the sale were taking longer than expected because some Turkcell executives have U.S. passports.[26] Then, in August 2008, Turkcell said it had frozen its plans for a venture in Syria amid U.S. opposition to the project. Makhluf's holding company, Cham, is involved in several other large deals, including an agreement with Syria's state airline and a Kuwaiti company to set up a new airline. Several months ago, Dubai-based real-estate company Emaar Properties announced it had agreed to set up a $100 million venture with Cham to develop real estate projects in Syria. Makhluf also is a minority shareholder in Gulfsands Petroleum,[27] a publicly traded, United Kingdom-incorporated energy company. According to the *Wall Street Journal*, a Gulfsands executive said the Treasury Department's sanctioning of Makhlouf would have no impact on the company pursuing its partnership with Cham.[28]

Sanctions against the Commercial Bank of Syria

As previously mentioned, under Section 311 of the USA PATRIOT Act, President Bush instructed the Treasury Department in 2004 to prepare a rule requiring U.S. financial institutions to sever correspondent accounts with the Commercial Bank of Syria because of money laundering concerns. In 2006, the Treasury Department issued a final ruling that imposes a special measure against the Commercial Bank of Syria as a financial institution of primary money laundering concern. It bars U.S. banks and their overseas subsidiaries from maintaining a correspondent account with the Commercial Bank of Syria, and it also requires banks to conduct due diligence that ensures the Commercial Bank of Syria is not circumventing sanctions through its business dealings with them.[29]

End Notes

1 In October, one prominent longtime activist, Haitham al Maleh, called for United Nations assistance but rejected help from NATO. According to Maleh, "NATO means America and I'm against that. But it's different when the Security Council intervenes. That provides an international umbrella, which is what is needed." See, U.S. Open Source Center (OSC)

Report GMP20111016637001, "Syria: Opposition Figure Al-Malih Supports International Intervention," *Al Akhbar* (Beirut), October 14, 2011.

[2] In September, three senior Alawite shaykhs in Homs issued a statement in which they said that the Asad regime does not represent their entire religious sect. OSC Report GMP20110912631001, "Syria: Three Alawite Figures Condemn 'Savage Acts,' Ask Syrians To Join Protests," *Al-Arabiyah.net* (Dubai), September 12, 2011.

[3] "Death Toll in Syria Mounts as Government Assault Continues," *New York Times*, November 8, 2011.

[4] In early October, Lebanon's Maronite Catholic Patriarch, Beshara al Rai, stated that hat he feared the collapse of "regimes described as dictatorial... could lead to civil war, with Christians being the main victims."

[5] On July 25, 2011, the Syrian government issued a bill that would permit the establishment of various new political parties. See, Syria: Bill Proposed to Allow New Political Parties, available online at: [http://www.loc.gov/lawweb/servlet/lloc_news?disp3_l205402 763_ text].

[6] "U.S. Cautions on Syria Deal, Says Assad Must Go," Reuters, November 2, 2011.

[7] "U.S. Doubts Military Option on Syria," Agence France Presse, October 24, 2011.

[8] "Fall of Syrian Regime a 'matter of time': U.S.," Agence France Presse, October 3, 2011.

[9] "Syria Cancels Fuel Export Tender, Sanctions Deter," Reuters, November 3, 2011.

[10] "Syrian Oil Exports Paralysed as Sanctions Bite," Reuters, September 22, 2011.

[11] "Syria looking for buyers after West rejects its oil," *International Herald Tribune*, September 29, 2011.

[12] Reuters, September 22, 2011, op.cit.

[13] Because of a number of legal restrictions and U.S. sanctions, many resulting from Syria's designation as a country supportive of international terrorism, Syria is no longer eligible to receive U.S. foreign assistance. Between 1950 and 1981, the United States provided a total of $627.4 million in aid to Syria: $34.0 million in development assistance, $438.0 million in economic support, and $155.4 million in food assistance. Most of this aid was provided during a brief warming trend in bilateral relations between 1974 and 1979. Significant projects funded under U.S. aid included water supply, irrigation, rural roads and electrification, and health and agricultural research. No aid has been provided to Syria since 1981, when the last aid programs were closed out.

[14] See, State Department Press Releases And Documents "Near East: Iran, North Korea, and Syria Nonproliferation Act: Imposed Sanctions," July 20, 2010.

[15] Syria's inclusion on the State Sponsors of Terrorism List as well as SALSA requires the president to restrict the export of any items to Syria that appear on the U.S. Munitions List (weapons, ammunition) or Commerce Control List (dual-use items).

[16] According to U.S. regulations, any product that contains more than 10% *de minimis* U.S.-origin content, regardless of where it is made, is not allowed to be exported to Syria. For U.S. commercial licensing prohibitions on exports and re-exports to Syria, see 15 C.F.R. pt. 736 Supp No. 1. The Department of Commerce reviews license applications on a case-by-case basis for exports or re-exports to Syria under a general policy of denial. For a description of items that do not require export licenses, see, Bureau of Industry and Security (BIS), U.S. Department of Commerce, Implementation of the Syria Accountability Act, available at http://www.bis.doc.gov/licensing/syriaimplementationmay14_04.htm.

[17] According to the original text of E.O. 13338, the president's authority to declare a national emergency authorizing the blocking of property of certain persons and prohibiting the exportation or re-exportation of certain goods to Syria is based on "The Constitution and the

laws of the United States of America, including the International Emergency Economic Powers Act (50 U.S.C. 1701 et seq.) (IEEPA), the National Emergencies Act (50 U.S.C. 1601 et seq.) (NEA), the Syria Accountability and Lebanese Sovereignty Restoration Act of 2003, P.L. 108-175 (SAA), and Section 301 of Title 3, United States Code." available at http://www.treasury.gov/resourcecenter/sanctions/Documents/13338.pdf.

[18] The president last extended the State of Emergency on April 29, 2011.

[19] See http://www.treasury.gov/press-center/press-releases/Pages/js2617.aspx.

[20] See http://www.treasury.gov/press-center/press-releases/Pages/hp60.aspx.

[21] See http://www.treasury.gov/press-center/press-releases/Pages/hp216.aspx .

[22] On July 29, 2010, President Obama extended that National Emergency with respect to Lebanon for another year, stating that "While there have been some recent positive developments in the Syrian-Lebanese relationship, continuing arms transfers to Hizballah that include increasingly sophisticated weapons systems serve to undermine Lebanese sovereignty, contribute to political and economic instability in Lebanon, and continue to pose an unusual and extraordinary threat to the national security and foreign policy of the United States." See, Notice of July 29, 2010— Continuation of the National Emergency With Respect to the Actions of Certain Persons to Undermine the Sovereignty of Lebanon or Its Democratic Processes and Institutions, Federal Register, Title 3—The president, [Page 45045].

[23] See http://www.treasury.gov/press-center/press-releases/Pages/hp666.aspx.

[24] A previous executive order, E.O. 13315, blocks property of former Iraqi President Saddam Hussein and members of his former regime. On June 9, 2005, the Treasury Department blocked property and interests of a Syrian company, SES International Corp., and two of its officials under the authority of E.O.13315.

[25] "Sanctions on Businessman Target Syria's Inner Sanctum," *Washington Post*, February 22, 2008.

[26] "Turkcell Continues Talks on Syriatel Stake," *Reuters*, April 14, 2008.

[27] Gulfsands' chief executive and largest shareholder, John Dorrier, is an American citizen, and the company has offices in Houston.

[28] " Syrian Tycoon Bristles At U.S. Sanctions Against Him," the *Wall Street Journal*, March 26, 2008.

[29] See, "U.S. Trade and Financial Sanctions Against Syria." Available at http://damascus. us embassy .gov/sanctionssyr.html.

INDEX

A

B

C

D

G

H

I

N

O

P

Q

R

S

T

U

V

W

Y